A Guide to the United States Constitution

SECOND EDITION

Erin Ackerman and Benjamin Ginsberg

A Guide to the United States Constitution

SECOND EDITION

Erin Ackerman
John Jay College–CUNY

Benjamin Ginsberg
The Johns Hopkins University

 W. W. NORTON & COMPANY • NEW YORK • LONDON

Copyright © 2011, 2007 by W. W. Norton & Company, Inc.

All rights reserved.

Second Edition.

Printed in the United States of America.

Composition and project management by Westchester Book Group.
Book design by Jack Meserole.
Project editor: Kim Yi.
Production manager: Ben Reynolds.
Manufacturing by Courier—Westford, MA.

Library of Congress Cataloging-in-Publication Data

Ackerman, Erin.
    A guide to the United States Constitution / Erin Ackerman, Benjamin Ginsberg. -- 2nd ed.
        p. cm.
    Ginsberg's name appears first on the earlier edition.
    Includes bibliographical references and index.
    ISBN 978-0-393-91288-3 (pbk.)
    1. United States. Constitution. 2. Constitutions--United States. 3. Constitutional law—United
States. 4. Law—United States--Interpretation and construction. 5. Constitutional history—United
States--Sources. I. Ginsberg, Benjamin. II. Title.
    KF4527.G56 2012
    342.7302--dc23

                                                                    2011025456

    W. W. Norton & Company, Inc., 500 Fifth Avenue, New York, N.Y. 10110
                        www.wwnorton.com
    W. W. Norton & Company Ltd., Castle House, 75/76 Wells Street, London W1T 3QT

    2 3 4 5 6 7 8 9 0

CONTENTS

Introduction: The Constitution and Constitution Day

The Constitution of the United States, adopted in 1787, is often said to be both the world's oldest written constitution and a continuing model for the nations of the world. Both of these assertions are only partly true. Nearly two millennia before the delegates to America's Constitutional Convention met in Philadelphia, a number of Greek city-states had produced written constitutions.* And, closer to home, all of the first American states possessed written constitutions. Nevertheless, it might be said that the U.S. Constitution was the first written document that formally organized the governmental processes of an entire nation. The Articles of Confederation, sometimes called America's first constitution, was more a compact among sovereign entities (the states) than an organic document for an entire nation.

As to the second assertion, the U.S. Constitution has served as a model for other nations. After America adopted its constitution in 1789, the idea of a written constitution gained considerable momentum. Both Poland and France adopted written constitutions in 1791, and over the next two centuries virtually every democracy developed a written constitution. The only exceptions today are Britain, Israel, and New Zealand. Indeed, possession of a constitution has become such an important attribute of political legitimacy that many despotic regimes have written constitutions—which they routinely ignore. Other national constitutions have copied features of the American model. Federalism and judicial review, for example, have been widely imitated. Most democracies, though, have opted for parliamentary governments rather than America's regime of separated executive and legislative powers. And most contemporary constitutions include extensive lists of political, social, cultural,

*Kim Lane Scheppele, "Constitutions Around the World," National Constitution Center, www.constitutioncenter.org/ncc_edu_constitutions_around_the_world.aspx.

1

and economic rights that have evolved in America via statute and the judicial process rather than constitutional mandate.

In 2004, Constitution Day became a federal holiday in the United States. Senator Robert Byrd sponsored an amendment to an omnibus spending bill that called for all educational institutions receiving federal funding to hold events and educational programming on September 17, the day on which, in 1787, the Founders signed the Constitution. The law was implemented in 2005 by the Department of Education, which announced that the requirement would apply to any school receiving federal funding of any kind. Rules announced in the Federal Register require schools to "hold an educational program pertaining to the United States Constitution on September 17 of each year."

In 2011, the new Republican majority of the 112th Congress began their session with a reading of the Constitution on the floor of the House of Representatives. The new majority also adopted a rule that all proposed legislation must include a citation to the portion of the Constitution that authorizes the legislation. Before the reading, members of the House debated which version of the Constitution to read. Ultimately they settled on reading the Constitution as amended and thus, not reading sections of the Constitution that have been changed, such as those that dealt with the maintenance of slavery in the early United States. Critics charged that this reading oversimplified the complicated history of the Constitution. During the reading of the Constitution, Republicans and Democrats alternated reading, with the House coming to a standing ovation for Representative John Lewis (D-GA), a leader of the Civil Rights Movement, who read the Thirteenth Amendment, which abolished slavery.

Members of the new majority, particularly those from the Tea Party movement, argued that the renewed attention to the Constitution was needed because Congress had in previous years exceeded the powers granted to it in the document, while the Democratic congressional minority argued that the framers had used broad language in order to allow for social and political change.

The Constitution of the United States

DRAFTING THE CONSTITUTION

Having declared their independence, the American colonies needed to establish a governmental structure. In November 1777, the Continental Congress adopted the Articles of Confederation and Perpetual Union—the United States' first constitution. The Articles of Confederation was the country's operative constitution until March 1789.

The main concern of the Articles of Confederation was to limit the powers of the central government. That central government under the Articles consisted entirely of a Congress with extremely limited power. Congressional delegates were really messengers from the state legislatures and were even paid out of state treasuries. Congress did not have the power to tax or regulate commerce and also had no centralized military, relying instead on the use of state militias. In effect, virtually all powers of government were retained by the individual states. This lack of centralized power negatively affected the ability of the Congress to negotiate with foreign nations and created economic instability domestically. The 1787 rebellion of farmers in Western Massachusetts against state government policies and pending foreclosure of their debt-ridden farms threw into relief the inability of the national government to intervene in a time of crisis and served as the catalyst for congressional support for revising the Articles of Confederation.

Delegates selected by the state governments convened in Philadelphia in May 1787. They soon abandoned plans to revise the Articles of Confederation, opting instead to create a new and, ultimately, vastly more effective form of national government. Authorship of the Constitution was a collaborative exercise. Few records exist that definitively identify particular authors for any specific section of the document.

The final Constitution most closely resembles the draft emerging from the Committee of Style, consisting of William Samuel Johnson (Connecticut), Alexander Hamilton (New York), Gouverneur Morris (Pennsylvania), James Madison (Virginia), and Rufus King (Massachusetts). The letters and papers of James Madison indicate that the document's literary style is largely that of Morris, although each and every portion of the document was submitted to the Convention for discussion and approval, which was, one can imagine, a time-intensive process.

PREAMBLE

[PREAMBLE]
> We the People of the United States, in Order to form a more perfect Union, establish Justice, insure domestic Tranquility, provide for the common defence, promote the general Welfare, and secure the Blessings of Liberty to ourselves and our Posterity, do ordain and establish this Constitution for the United States of America.

The Preamble does not create any substantive powers of the new government, but rather sets out its purposes and general principles. The concerns of American society at the time are evident in the wording used for the Preamble. The opening, "We the People," emphasizes an appeal to popular opinion. In the aftermath of Shays's Rebellion, Convention delegates, who mostly came from the elite of American society, were particularly concerned with having the approval of the common person, while also channeling popular sentiment. Indeed, violent incidents like Shays's Rebellion and the political dissatisfaction that prompted them were foremost in the minds of the Founders and Americans generally, a concern that is echoed in the hopes for establishing Peace, Justice, and domestic Tranquility. The Preamble's wording of a *more* Perfect Union invokes the need to improve on the deficiencies of the Articles of Confederation.

ARTICLE I

Article I outlines the composition and responsibilities of the legislative branch. It provides for a Congress consisting of two chambers—a House of Representatives and a Senate—and then outlines the powers of the national legislature.

Section 1

[LEGISLATIVE POWERS]
> All legislative Powers herein granted shall be vested in a Congress of the United States, which shall consist of a Senate and House of Representatives.

Article I, Section 1, provides for the creation of a Congress of the United States and stipulates that the Congress will be the federal government's lawmaking body. The

Congress is **bicameral**; it is divided into two chambers—a Senate and House of Representatives. Before a proposal can become law, it must be approved by both houses of Congress and signed by the president (Section 7). The framers hoped that each chamber would serve as a check on unwise or ill-conceived actions by the other. They believed that constructing separate institutions to exercise the major powers of government and creating means through which each could be checked by the others would prevent undue concentrations of power and protect the nation from arbitrary and tyrannical actions on the part of the government. Concerns about containing government power and restraining "excessive democracy," sudden shifts in public opinion, are what drove the particular configuration of the national government under the Constitution. James Madison, one of the principal authors of the Constitution, said in *Federalist 51* that the separate parts of the government would work to keep each other in their proper places. Thus, separation of powers and checks and balances are at the heart of America's constitutional structure. From the framers' perspective, occasional inefficiency in decision making was part of the price to be paid for liberty.

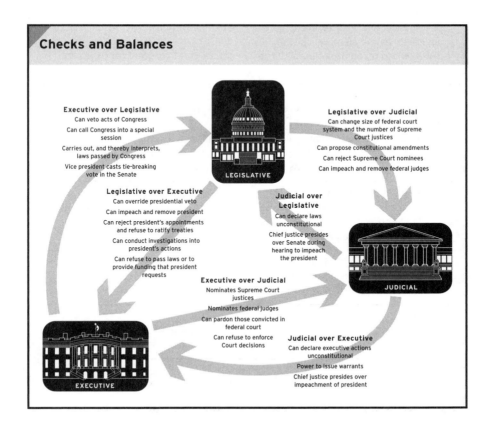

Checks and Balances

Executive over Legislative
Can veto acts of Congress
Can call Congress into a special session
Carries out, and thereby interprets, laws passed by Congress
Vice president casts tie-breaking vote in the Senate

Legislative over Judicial
Can change size of federal court system and the number of Supreme Court justices
Can propose constitutional amendments
Can reject Supreme Court nominees
Can impeach and remove federal judges

LEGISLATIVE

Legislative over Executive
Can override presidential veto
Can impeach and remove president
Can reject president's appointments and refuse to ratify treaties
Can conduct investigations into president's actions
Can refuse to pass laws or to provide funding that president requests

Judicial over Legislative
Can declare laws unconstitutional
Chief justice presides over Senate during hearing to impeach the president

Executive over Judicial
Nominates Supreme Court justices
Nominates federal judges
Can pardon those convicted in federal court
Can refuse to enforce Court decisions

Judicial over Executive
Can declare executive actions unconstitutional
Power to issue warrants
Chief justice presides over impeachment of president

JUDICIAL

EXECUTIVE

6 | *A Guide to the United States Constitution*

The Seven Articles of the Constitution

1. The Legislative Branch
   House: two-year terms, elected directly by the people.
   Senate: six-year terms (staggered so that only one-third of the Senate changes in any given election), appointed by state legislature (changed in 1913 to direct election).
   Expressed powers of the national government: collecting taxes, borrowing money, regulating commerce, declaring war, and maintaining an army and a navy; all other power belongs to the states, unless deemed otherwise by the elastic (necessary and proper) clause.
   Exclusive powers of the national government: states are expressly forbidden to issue their own paper money, tax imports and exports, regulate trade outside their own borders, and impair the obligation of contracts; these powers are the exclusive domain of the national government.

2. The Executive Branch
   Presidency: four-year terms (limited in 1951 to a maximum of two terms), elected indirectly by the electoral college.
   Powers: can recognize other countries, negotiate treaties, grant reprieves and pardons, convene Congress in special sessions, and veto congressional enactment.

3. The Judicial Branch
   Supreme Court: lifetime terms, appointed by the president with the approval of the Senate.
   Powers: include resolving conflicts between federal and state laws, determining whether power belongs to the national government or the states, and settling controversies between citizens of different states.

4. National Unity and Power
   Reciprocity among states: establishes that each state must give "full faith and credit" to official acts of other states, and guarantees citizens of any state the "privileges and immunities" of every other state.

5. Amending the Constitution
   Procedure: requires approval by two-thirds of Congress and adoption by three-fourths of the states.

6. National Supremacy
   The Constitution and national law are the supreme law of the land and cannot be overruled by state law.

7. Ratification
   The Constitution became effective when approved by nine states.

Section 2

[HOUSE OF REPRESENTATIVES, HOW CONSTITUTED, POWER OF IMPEACHMENT]

The House of Representatives shall be composed of Members chosen every second Year by the People of the several States, and the Electors in each State shall have the Qualifications requisite for Electors of the most numerous Branch of the State Legislature.

No Person shall be a Representative who shall not have attained to the Age of twenty five Years, and been seven Years a Citizen of the United States, and who shall not, when elected, be an Inhabitant of that State in which he shall be chosen.

Representatives and *direct Taxes*[1] shall be apportioned among the several States which may be included within this Union, according to their respective Numbers, *which shall be determined by adding to the whole Number of free Persons, including those bound to Service for a Term of Years, and excluding Indians not taxed, three fifths of all other Persons.*[2] The actual Enumeration shall be made within three Years after the first Meeting of the Congress of the United States, and within every subsequent Term of ten Years, in such Manner as they shall by Law direct. The Number of Representatives shall not exceed one for every thirty Thousand, but each State shall have at Least one Representative; *and until such enumeration shall be made, the State of New Hampshire shall be entitled to choose three, Massachusetts eight, Rhode-Island and providence Plantations one, Connecticut five, New-York six, New Jersey four, Pennsylvania eight, Delaware one, Maryland six, Virginia ten, North Carolina five, South Carolina five, and Georgia three.*[3]

When vacancies happen in the Representation from any State, the Executive Authority thereof shall issue Writs of Election to fill such Vacancies.

The House of Representatives shall chuse their Speaker and other Officers; and shall have the sole Power of ImPeachment.

Perhaps the most divisive issue in the creation of the new government was that of determining the best form of representation in the national legislature. At the start of the convention, Edmund Randolph of Virginia offered a plan in which representation in the national legislature would be based on the population of each state or the proportion of the state's revenue contribution to the national government, or both. Termed the "Virginia Plan," this proposal was thought to favor large states and thus was distrusted by delegates from the smaller states. They made their opposition known in a resolution introduced by William Paterson of New Jersey. In what would become known as the "New Jersey Plan," delegates proposed that each state be equally represented in the new regime regardless of population or revenue.

Section 2 is the result of the "Great Compromise," by which this dispute was settled. Representation in the House was based on population, while in the Senate (Section 3) each state would have two members. Note that while they are officials of the national government, senators and representatives speak for states or districts within states. The Constitution creates a national government but does not erase state boundaries. Hence, our government is a federal government, not a unitary national regime.

[1]Modified by Sixteenth Amendment.
[2]Modified by Fourteenth Amendment.
[3]Temporary provision.

The most important provisions of Section 2 concern the selection of members of the House of Representatives. At the Constitutional Convention, some delegates were fearful of what they called "excessive democracy" and argued against direct popular election of public officials. Other delegates thought that voting should be restricted to individuals who possessed a certain amount of property or income. Many influential delegates, however, pointed out that most of the states allowed ordinary citizens to choose the members of the lower houses of their legislatures. These delegates argued that citizens would not trust or support the federal government if they believed that they had more influence at the state level. This argument carried the day. Hence the Constitution stipulates that in every state anyone eligible to cast a ballot for members of the lower house of their own state legislature is also eligible to vote for members of Congress.

Members of the House serve two-year terms. The framers thought this length of term would keep representatives close to their constituents but still give them enough time to master the business of government.

Also included in Section 2 is the infamous Three-Fifths Compromise. Delegates from the slaveholding states demanded to be allowed to count slaves in determining the number of representatives to which states would be entitled. Delegates from the free states rejected this idea. Under the compromise formula, the number of representatives to which a state was entitled would be based on its entire free population plus three-fifths of its slave population. This section became moot in 1868 with the ratification of the Thirteenth Amendment, ending slavery.

In addition to establishing rules for the selection of members, Section 2 gives the House of Representatives two important powers. First, the House is empowered to choose its "Speaker and other officers." This provision enhances the House's control of its own procedures and affairs. This control is broad and includes the House setting its own ethics rules. The outer boundaries of this power were identi-

Differences between the House and the Senate

	HOUSE	SENATE
Minimum age of member	25 years	30 years
U.S. citizenship	At least 7 years	At least 9 years
Length of term	2 years	6 years
Number representing each state	1–53 (depends on population)	2 per state
Constituency	Tends to be local	Both local and national

fied in *Powell v. McCormack* (1969), in which the Supreme Court held that while the House has discretion over its internal procedures, it could not refuse to seat a lawfully elected member for reasons other than age, citizenship, and residence as outlined in Article I, Section 2.

Section 2 also assigns to the House the power of impeachment. Impeachment is the power to bring charges against a governmental official and to call for his or her removal from office. In the course of American history, two presidents—Andrew Johnson and Bill Clinton—one Supreme Court Justice—Samuel Chase—and several federal judges have been impeached by the House. Of these officials, only a few of the lower federal court judges have been removed from office. The power to try impeachments is granted to the Senate, where a two-thirds majority is needed for conviction (Section 3).

Section 3

[THE SENATE, HOW CONSTITUTED, IMPEACHMENT TRIALS]

The Senate of the United States shall be composed of two Senators from each State, *chosen by the Legislature thereof,*[4] for six Years; and each Senator shall have one Vote.

Immediately after they shall be assembled in Consequence of the first Election, they shall be divided as equally as may be into three Classes. The Seats of the Senators of the first Class shall be vacated at the Expiration of the second Year, of the second Class at the Expiration of the fourth Year, and of the third Class at the Expiration of the sixth Year, so that one third may be chosen every second Year; *and if Vacancies happen by Resignation, or otherwise, during the Recess of the Legislature of any State, the Executive thereof may make temporary Appointments until the next Meeting of the Legislature, which shall then fill such Vacancies.*[5]

No Person shall be a Senator who shall not have attained to the Age of thirty Years, and been nine Years a Citizen of the United States, and who shall not, when elected, be an Inhabitant of that State for which he shall be chosen.

The Vice President of the United States shall be President of the Senate, but shall have no Vote, unless they be equally divided.

The Senate shall chuse their other Officers, and also a President pro tempore, in the Absence of the Vice President, or when he shall exercise the Office of President of the United States.

The Senate shall have the sole Power to try all Impeachments. When sitting for that Purpose, they shall be on Oath or Affirmation. When the President of the United States is tried, the Chief Justice shall preside: And no Person shall be convicted without the Concurrence of two thirds of the Members present.

Judgment in Cases of Impeachment shall not extend further than to removal from Office, and disqualification to hold and enjoy any Office of honor, Trust or Profit under the United States: but the Party convicted shall nevertheless be liable and subject to Indictment, Trial, Judgment and Punishment, according to Law.

[4]Modified by Seventeenth Amendment.
[5]Modified by Seventeenth Amendment.

This section of Article I prescribes the manner in which senators are to be chosen. Each state is entitled to two senators. Initially, senators were appointed by the state legislatures. The Senate was originally intended to check mass democracy by balancing the popular election of the House of Representatives with the appointment of senators charged with representing the state at large. The Seventeenth Amendment, however, ratified in 1913, provided for popular election of senators.

Section 3 stipulates that senators serve six-year terms in office. The framers thought that long terms for senators would make the Senate a more deliberative body than the House. Six-year terms would allow senators to withstand constituency pressures and make independent judgments on the basis of what they thought was right rather than what they knew to be popular. Also designed to make the Senate a deliberative body was the principle of staggered terms. Every two years, a third of the senators face reelection while the others continue serving their terms and are not in danger of being forced from office. This means that at any point in time, most senators do not have to worry immediately about their popularity and its electoral consequences.

Section 4

[ELECTION OF SENATORS AND REPRESENTATIVES]

    The Times, Places and Manner of holding Elections for Senators and Representatives, shall be prescribed in each State by the Legislature thereof; but the Congress may at any time by Law make or alter such Regulations, except as to the Places of chusing Senators.

    The Congress shall assemble at least once in every Year, and such Meeting shall be on the first Monday in December, unless they shall by Law appoint a different Day.[6]

This Section has been superseded by the Twentieth Amendment (1933), which fixes the terms of members of Congress and the timing of congressional sessions. Congress has also enacted a number of statutes diminishing state authority in this area.

Section 5

[QUORUM, JOURNALS, MEETINGS, ADJOURNMENTS]

    Each House shall be the Judge of the Elections, Returns and Qualifications of its own Members, and a Majority of each shall constitute a Quorum to do Business; but a smaller Number may adjourn from day to day, and may be authorized to compel the Attendance of absent Members, in such Manner, and under such Penalties as each House may provide.

    Each House may determine the Rules of its Proceedings, punish its Members for disorderly Behaviour, and, with the Concurrence of two thirds, expel a Member.

    Each House shall keep a Journal of its Proceedings, and from time to time publish the same, excepting such Parts as may in their Judgment require Secrecy; and the Yeas and Nays of the Members of either House on any questions shall, at the Desire of one fifth of those Present, be entered on the Journal.

---

[6]Modified by Twentieth Amendment.

Neither House, during the Session of Congress, shall, without the Consent of the other, adjourn for more than three days, nor to any other Place than that in which the two Houses shall be sitting.

Congress determines its own rules and procedures and determines whether individuals are entitled to serve as members. As mentioned earlier, however, in doing this, Congress cannot disregard the expressed wishes of the electors. In 1966 the House refused to permit Adam Clayton Powell, a famous black representative, to take the seat to which he had been reelected by his Harlem constituency. Powell had served in Congress for many years and was chair of the powerful House Labor and Education Committee. In the 1960s, Powell came under investigation for improper use of congressional funds, excessive absenteeism, and failure to pay a slander judgment in his home district. The House voted, 307 to 116, to exclude him and declare his seat vacant. In *Powell v. McCormack* (1969), the Supreme Court held that while the House has discretion over its internal procedures, it cannot refuse to seat a lawfully elected member for reasons other than those listed in the text of the Constitution—age, citizenship, and residence—outlined in Article I, Section 2. Powell was reelected by his constituents while the case was pending. Instead of attempting to exclude him again, the House voted to strip him of his seniority and committee chairmanship.

As required by Section 5, Congress also keeps records of its proceedings, mainly in the *Congressional Record*. This daily report of the debates and actions of Congress is made available to the public through the Government Printing Office (GPO), the Federal Depository Library Program, and, increasingly, online through the Federal Digital System (FDSys).

Section 6

[COMPENSATION, PRIVILEGES, DISABILITIES]

The Senators and Representatives shall receive a Compensation for their Services, to be ascertained by Law, and paid out of the Treasury of the United States. They shall in all Cases, except Treason, Felony and Breach of the Peace, be privileged from Arrest during their Attendance at the Session of their respective Houses, and in going to and returning from the same; and for any Speech or Debate in either House, they shall not be questioned in any other Place.

No Senator or Representative shall, during the Time for which he was elected, be appointed to any civil Office under the Authority of the United States, which shall have been created, or the Emoluments whereof shall have been encreased during such time; and no Person holding any Office under the United States, shall be a Member of either House during his Continuance in Office.

Currently, congressional salaries are set under a procedure adopted by Congress in 1989. If Congress chooses to change the formula governing congressional pay, the Twenty-Seventh Amendment (1992) provides that the new pay scale cannot take effect until after the next election. This amendment was intended to guard against self-serving behavior on the part of members. In 2011, members received an annual salary of $174,000.

Section 6 also provides that members of Congress cannot be punished for their words, opinions, or actions in connection with performance of their legislative duties. This provision is necessary to allow members to take unpopular positions and to oppose the executive branch. The Supreme Court, however, held in the 1972 case of *United States v. Brewster* that a member whose congressional activities stem from criminal activity—such as the acceptance of bribes—is not immune from prosecution.

Section 7

[PROCEDURE IN PASSING BILLS AND RESOLUTIONS]

All Bills for raising Revenue shall originate in the House of Representatives; but the Senate may propose or concur with Amendments as on other Bills.

Every Bill which shall have passed the House of Representatives and the Senate, shall, before it become a Law, be presented to the President of the United States: If he approve he shall sign it, but if not he shall return it, with his Objections to that House in which it shall have originated, who shall enter the Objections at large on their Journal, and proceed to reconsider it. If after such Reconsideration two thirds of that House shall agree to pass the Bill, it shall be sent, together with the Objections, to the other House, by which it shall likewise be reconsidered, and if approved by two thirds of that House, it shall become a Law. But in all such Cases the Votes of both Houses shall be determined by yeas and Nays, and the Names of the Persons voting for and against the Bill shall be entered on the Journal of each House respectively. If any Bill shall not be returned by the President within ten Days (Sundays excepted) after it shall have been presented to him, the Same shall be a Law, in like Manner as if he had signed it, unless the Congress by their Adjournment prevent its Return, in which Case it shall not be a Law.

Every Order, Resolution, or Vote to which the Concurrence of the Senate and House of Representatives may be necessary (except on a question of Adjournment) shall be presented to the President of the United States; and before the Same shall take Effect, shall be approved by him, or being disapproved by him, shall be repassed by two thirds of the Senate and House of Representatives, according to the Rules and Limitations prescribed in the Case of a Bill.

To become a law, every bill must be approved by both houses of Congress and signed by the president. This is a key example of the constitutional principle of checks and balances. With one exception, bills may originate in either house of Congress. Tax bills must originate in the House. The framers thought it was important to give this special authority to the more popular house of Congress.

The second and third clauses of this section are known as the "presentment clause." If a bill has been passed by the House and Senate, it is presented to the president, who has ten days in which to sign or veto the bill. If the president takes no action, the bill becomes law without his signature unless the Congress has adjourned, in which case the bill does not take effect. If the president vetoes the bill, a two-thirds majority of both houses of Congress is required to override the president's objections. In 1998, the Supreme Court ruled in *Clinton v. City of New York* that a presidential line item veto violates the presentment clause.

Section 8

[POWERS OF CONGRESS]

The Congress shall have Power

To lay and collect Taxes, Duties, Imposts and Excises, to pay the Debts and provide for the common Defence and general Welfare of the United States; but all Duties, Imposts and Excises shall be uniform throughout the United States;

To borrow Money on the credit of the United States;

To regulate Commerce with foreign Nations, and among the several States, and with the Indian Tribes;

To establish an uniform Rule of Naturalization, and uniform Laws on the subject of Bankruptcies throughout the United States;

To coin Money, regulate the Value thereof, and of foreign Coin, and fix the Standard of Weights and Measures;

To provide for the Punishment of counterfeiting the Securities and current Coin of the United States;

To establish Post Offices and post Roads;

To promote the Progress of Science and useful Arts, by securing for limited Times to Authors and Inventors the exclusive Right to their respective Writings and Discoveries;

To constitute Tribunals inferior to the supreme Court;

To define and punish Piracies and Felonies committed on the high Seas, and Offences against the Law of Nations;

To declare War, grant Letters of Marque and Reprisal, and make Rules concerning Captures on Land and Water;

To raise and support Armies, but no Appropriation of Money to that Use shall be for a longer Term than two Years;

To provide and maintain a Navy;

To make Rules for the Government and Regulation of the land and naval Forces;

To provide for calling forth the Militia to execute the Laws of the Union, suppress Insurrections and repel Invasions;

To provide for organizing, arming, and disciplining, the Militia, and for governing such Part of them as may be employed in the Service of the United States, reserving to the States respectively, the Appointment of the Officers, and the Authority of training the Militia according to the discipline prescribed by Congress;

To exercise exclusive Legislation in all Cases whatsoever, over such District (not exceeding ten Miles square) as may, by Cession of particular States, and the Acceptance of Congress, become the Seat of the Government of the United States, and to exercise like Authority over all Places purchased by the Consent of the Legislature of the State in which the Same shall be, for the Erection of Forts, Magazines, Arsenals, dock-Yards, and other needful Buildings;—And

To make all Laws which shall be necessary and proper for carrying into Execution the foregoing Powers, and all other Powers vested by this Constitution in the Government of the United States, or in any Department or Officer thereof.

Section 8 is the heart of the Constitution. It lists the **expressed powers** of Congress and, in effect, enumerates the powers of the federal government. Our government is one of enumerated powers. That is, the government's power is not unlimited. The Constitution defines the powers that the federal government may exercise and implies that it grants only those powers that are expressed in the text—that powers not listed are not granted at all.

Nevertheless, the framers had learned from the experience of the Articles of Confederation that they needed an active and powerful government. Thus, Section 8 contains an expansive list of federal powers. And the last paragraph of Section 8, sometimes called the **elastic clause**, avers that Congress has the power to make laws that are "necessary and proper" for implementing the powers granted to it. Its enumerated powers, coupled with the elastic clause, give the federal government an important array of tools to use to govern the country.

Among the most important congressional powers enumerated in Section 8 is the power to regulate commerce "with foreign Nations, and among the several States, and with the Indian Tribes." Under the Articles of Confederation, the national government lacked substantive power to regulate commerce, and the new Constitution intended to remedy this limitation. The commerce provisions of the Constitution were adopted with relative ease by the Convention and occasioned little Antifederalist protest during the ratification debates. This indicates substantial consensus on the need for enhanced national power in the area of commerce.

The interstate aspect of the commerce clause has been one of the most litigated clauses of the entire Constitution. Since Chief Justice John Marshall's expansive interpretation of the commerce power in *Gibbons v. Ogden* (1824), the commerce clause has been the main constitutional basis on which Congress intervenes in domestic life. In *Gibbons*, the Court overturned a New York State law that granted a monopoly on New York waters to Robert Fulton's steamboat company. Marshall outlined a broad concept of interstate commerce, stating that the "power to regulate commerce extends to every species of commercial intercourse between the United States and foreign nations, and among the several States." According to Marshall, "among" meant "intermingled with," and thus activities affecting interstate commerce fell under the jurisdiction of this clause even if they seemed to be physically contained within state borders. The power of Congress to regulate interstate commerce, according to *Gibbons*, "does not stop at the external boundary of a State." Marshall stopped just short of giving Congress exclusive power over commerce, reserving that commerce that was "completely internal" should remain under the regulation of states and that states could regulate commerce in the absence of federal laws.

Prior to and in the beginning of the Industrial Revolution, however, the Court emphasized the dual responsibilities of the state and national governments in this area. Justices appointed by Presidents Jackson and Van Buren limited the range of activities that could be considered interstate commerce, particularly activities within state borders. Subsequent jurisprudence emphasized the popular notions of laissez-faire economics and Social Darwinism and resulted in obstacles to congressional power in addressing the consequences of industrialization. From about 1890 to 1937, the Court developed several doctrines that increasingly obstructed Congress's power to regulate commerce in the age of industrialization. Among these were the drawing of a distinction between production/manufacturing and commerce, which led to the finding that Congress could only regulate the interstate movement of manufactured goods, not their production; the argument that Congress could regulate only the direct effects of commerce, not its indirect effects; and the deferring to the doctrine of "dual federalism," under which congressional commerce power was limited by the powers reserved to the states in the Tenth Amendment (*United States v. E. C. Knight Co.* [1895], *Hammer v. Dagenhart* [1918], *Carter v. Carter Coal Co.* [1936], *Schechter Poultry Corp. v. United States* [1935]). On these grounds, the Court invalidated many of President Franklin D. Roosevelt's initial New Deal programs, prompting the president to propose his infamous Court-packing plan. The plan failed, but many believe it contributed to the "switch in time that saved Nine," also called the "New Deal Consensus"—a shift in judicial philosophy that restored to Congress a broad power to regulate any "class of activities" that affects commerce, including production and labor standards (*West Coast Hotel v. Parrish* [1937], *United States v. Darby Lumber Co.* [1941], *Wickard v. Filburn* [1942]). Now when Congress enacts legislation affecting highway safety, the environment, racial discrimination, health, and so forth, it generally claims that its authority stems from its power to regulate commerce between the states. After the Obama administration's health insurance reform was signed into law in 2010, several states and some business groups challenged its constitutionality in court. The states and business groups argued that the law exceeded Congress's power to regulate interstate commerce. As of early 2011, four different federal district courts had ruled on suits challenging the law. Two of the courts upheld the law as within Congress's commerce power, while two found that Congress had overreached.

Another important power that Section 8 gives Congress is the power to declare war. Many of the framers believed that by giving this power to Congress rather than the president they would render the nation less likely to initiate military action against other nations. The last time Congress declared war was December 8, 1941, but U.S. troops have been sent into action many times since that date. In recent decades, presidents have argued that Congress's war powers are not relevant to modern military and security actions and have initiated action on their own authority as commander in chief. In 1973, Congress enacted the War Powers Act to limit presidential use of military force without congressional authorization, but this act has not proved to be a functional limit on presidents and Congress has largely complied with presidential use of military force.

Section 9

[SOME RESTRICTIONS ON FEDERAL POWER]

The Migration or Importation of such Persons as any of the States now existing shall think proper to admit, shall not be prohibited by the Congress prior to the Year one thousand eight hundred and eight, but a Tax or duty may be imposed on such Importation, not exceeding ten dollars for each Person.[7]

The Privilege of the Writ of Habeas Corpus shall not be suspended, unless when in Cases of Rebellion or Invasion the public Safety may require it.

No Bill of Attainder or ex post facto Law shall be passed.

No Capitation, or other direct, Tax shall be laid, unless in Proportion to the Census or Enumeration herein before directed to be taken.[8]

No Tax or Duty shall be laid on Articles exported from any State.

No Preference shall be given by any Regulation of Commerce or Revenue to the Ports of one State over those of another; nor shall Vessels bound to, or from, one State, be obliged to enter, clear, or pay Duties in another.

No Money shall be drawn from the Treasury, but in Consequence of Appropriations made by Law; and a regular Statement and Account of the Receipts and Expenditures of all public Money shall be published from time to time.

No Title of Nobility shall be granted by the United States: And no Person holding any Office of Profit or Trust under them, shall, without the Consent of the Congress, accept of any present, Emolument, Office, or Title, of any kind whatever, from any King, Prince, or foreign State.

This section places some restrictions on federal power. The most important is the provision for a writ of habeas corpus, which allows a judge to inquire into the legality of deprivation of personal liberty. The most familiar form of loss of liberty is the arbitrary arrest of those whom the authorities suspect of crimes, but it can take many forms, including commitment to a mental institution or forced military service. In responding to a writ, or petition, of habeas corpus, a judge inquires into whether an individual has been illegally detained or otherwise deprived of personal liberty. For example, an individual taken into custody by federal authorities must be charged before a magistrate or released.

Times of emergency have prompted presidents and Congress to argue for the temporary suspension of the writ of habeas corpus. Abraham Lincoln suspended the writ of habeas corpus during the Civil War, a move that Congress eventually authorized by statute. This suspension resulted in the cases of *Ex parte Merryman* (1861) and *Ex parte Milligan* (1866). In these cases, the justices determined that the president lacks the authority to suspend habeas corpus, but the cases achieved little real change; Lincoln continued the practice even after *Merryman*; the decision in *Milligan* was handed down only after the end of the war. In another example, the terrorism legislation enacted by Congress in September 2006, known as the "Military Commissions Act of 2006," took away the right of habeas corpus from foreigners held by American

[7]Temporary provision.
[8]Modified by Sixteenth Amendment.

authorities and designated by the president as enemy combatants. In 2007, however, the Supreme Court ruled in *Boumediene v. Bush* that the alternate legal procedures established by the Military Commissions Act were an inadequate substitute for the judicial review protections of habeas corpus. Every state constitution also provides for habeas corpus where state authorities are involved.

Section 9 also prohibits bills of attainder and ex post facto laws. A bill of attainder is a legislative act punishing an individual without a trial. An ex post facto law is one written to apply to prior acts that were legal at the time.

As a result of pressure from delegates from the slaveholding states, Section 9 also prohibits the federal government from interfering with the importation of slaves before 1808. This section was superseded by the Thirteenth Amendment.

Section 10

[RESTRICTIONS UPON POWERS OF STATES]
   No State shall enter into any Treaty, Alliance, or Confederation; grant Letters of Marque and Reprisal; coin Money; emit Bills of Credit; make any Thing but gold and silver Coin a Tender in Payment of Debts; pass any Bill of Attainder, ex post facto Law, or Law impairing the Obligation of Contracts, or grant any Title of Nobility.
   No State shall, without the Consent of the Congress, lay any Imposts or Duties on Imports or Exports, except what may be absolutely necessary for executing its inspection Laws: and the net Produce of all Duties and Imposts, laid by any State on Imports or Exports, shall be for the Use of the Treasury of the United States; and all such Laws shall be subject to the Revision and Control of the Congress.
   No State shall, without the Consent of Congress, lay any Duty of Tonnage, keep Troops, or Ships of War in time of Peace, enter into any Agreement or Compact with another State, or with a foreign Power, or engage in War, unless actually invaded, or in such imminent Danger as will not admit of delay.

Section 8 provides the federal government with a number of important powers. Section 10 prohibits the states from exercising a number of these same powers, such as coining money or signing treaties with foreign nations. Taken together, Sections 8 and 10 transfer significant powers from the state to the national level.

ARTICLE II

America's government under the Articles of Confederation had no executive institutions. This was a source of national governmental weakness that the framers were determined to overcome. Hence the Constitution creates the presidency and vests the executive power in the occupant of the office. Some convention delegates favored a multiperson executive to avoid undue concentration of power in one individual, but most thought that a single decisive individual would help to energize the federal government and allow it to operate more effectively and efficiently.

Since the adoption of the Constitution, Congress has created numerous governmental agencies that also exercise executive power. Congress attempts to monitor the operations of these agencies through a process called "oversight," which Congress believes is implied by the theory of checks and balances. Proponents of presidential power, however, point to the language of Article II, which vests executive power in the president. They say this implies that the executive agencies work for the president and should not be subject to direct congressional oversight. This is known as the idea of the "unitary executive."

Section 1

[EXECUTIVE POWER, ELECTION, QUALIFICATIONS OF THE PRESIDENT]
 The executive Power shall be vested in a President of the United States of America. *He shall hold his Office during the Term of four Years, and, together with the Vice President, chosen for the same Term, be elected, as follows*[9]
 Each State shall appoint, in such Manner as the Legislature thereof may direct, a Number of Electors, equal to the whole Number of Senators and Representatives to which the State may be entitled in the Congress: but no Senator or Representative, or Person holding an Office of Trust or Profit under the United States, shall be appointed an Elector.
 The electors shall meet in their respective States, and vote by ballot for two Persons, of whom one at least shall not be an Inhabitant of the same State with themselves. And they shall make a List of all the Persons voted for, and of the Number of Votes for each; which List they shall sign and certify, and transmit sealed to the Seat of the Government of the United States, directed to the President of the Senate. The President of the Senate shall, in the Presence of the Senate and House of Representatives, open all the Certificates, and the Votes shall then be counted. The Person having the greatest Number of Votes shall be the President, if such Number be a Majority of the whole Number of Electors appointed; and if there be more than one who have such Majority, and have an equal Number of Votes, then the House of Representatives shall immediately chuse by Ballot one of them for President; and if no Person have a Majority, then from the five highest on the List the said House shall in like Manner chuse the President. But in chusing the President, the Votes shall be taken by States, the Representation from each State having one Vote; A quorum for this Purpose shall consist of a Member or Members from two thirds of the States, and a Majority of all the States shall be necessary to a Choice. In every Case, after the Choice of the President, the person having the greatest Number of Votes of the Electors shall be the Vice President. But if there should remain two or more who have equal Votes, the Senate shall chuse from them by Ballot the Vice President.[10]
 The Congress may determine the Time of chusing the Electors, and the Day on which they shall give their Votes; which Day shall be the same throughout the United States.
 No Person except a natural born Citizen, or a Citizen of the United States, at the time of the Adoption of this Constitution, shall be eligible to the Office of President; neither shall any Person be eligible to that Office who shall not have attained to the Age of thirty five Years, and been fourteen Years a Resident within the United States.
 In Case of the Removal of the President from Office, or his Death, Resignation, or Inability to discharge the Powers and Duties of the said Office, the Same shall devolve on the

[9]Number of terms limited to two by Twenty-Second Amendment.
[10]Modified by Twelfth and Twentieth Amendments.

Vice President, and the Congress may by Law provide for the Case of Removal, Death, Resignation or Inability, both of the President and Vice President, declaring what Officer shall then act as President, and such Officer shall act accordingly, until the Disability be removed, or a President shall be elected.

The President shall, at stated Times, receive for his Services, a Compensation, which shall neither be increased nor diminished during the Period for which he shall have been elected, and he shall not receive within that Period any other Emolument from the United States, or any of them.

Before he enter on the Execution of his Office, he shall take the following Oath or Affirmation:—"I do solemnly swear (or affirm) that I will faithfully execute the Office of President of the United States, and will to the best of my Ability, preserve, protect and defend the Constitution of the United States."

Section 1 creates a presidential election system that has been substantially changed over the years. Under the original system, each state legislature appointed presidential electors who met in their respective states and cast ballots for president and vice president. In the event that no one won a majority in the electoral college, something that was likely given the fragmented character of the electoral process, Congress would select the president. Today, every state's presidential electors are chosen by direct popular vote. The electors present themselves in partisan slates and have all pledged to cast their vote for their party's presidential nominee. The slate of electors that wins in a state casts all of the state's votes for its party's presidential candidate. Under this system, it is still possible, but not likely, that an election will end without a majority in the Electoral College, which would leave the final decision to the Congress. Depending on the distribution of outcomes across the states, it is also possible for the winner in the Electoral College to be someone other than the candidate who received the most popular votes. This happened most recently in 2000, when George W. Bush lost the popular contest but won in the Electoral College after the Supreme Court in *Bush v. Gore* awarded him Florida's disputed electoral votes.

Section 1 also outlines the minimum qualifications for the presidency—it provides that in order to be eligible to be president a person must be a natural-born citizen of the United States, must be at least thirty-five years old, and must have resided in the United States for fourteen years. And Section 1 sets out the exact wording of the Oath of Office. At the inauguration of Barack Obama in January 2009, one word in the oath of office was said out of order by Chief Justice John Roberts and then by Obama. Because the Constitution sets out the exact oath, the day after the inauguration, the Chief Justice came to the White House to readminister the oath of office to President Obama, just in case.

Section 2

[POWERS OF THE PRESIDENT]

The President shall be Commander in Chief of the Army and Navy of the United States, and of the Militia of the several States, when called into the actual Service of the United

States; he may require the Opinion, in writing, of the principal Officer in each of the executive Departments, upon any Subject relating to the Duties of their respective Offices, and he shall have Power to grant Reprieves and Pardons for Offences against the United States, except in Cases of Impeachment.

He shall have Power, by and with the Advice and Consent of the Senate, to make Treaties, provided two thirds of the Senators present concur; and he shall nominate, and by and with the Advice and Consent of the Senate, shall appoint Ambassadors, other public Ministers and Consuls, Judges of the supreme Court, and all other Officers of the United States, whose Appointments are not herein otherwise provided for, and which shall be established by Law: but the Congress may by Law vest the Appointment of such inferior Officers, as they think proper, in the President alone, in the Courts of Law, or in the Heads of Departments.

The President shall have Power to fill up all Vacancies that may happen during the Recess of the Senate, by granting Commissions which shall expire at the End of their next Session.

This section outlines the powers to be exercised by the president. The president is given the unconditional power to accept ambassadors from other countries; this amounts to the power to "recognize" other countries. The president is also given the power to negotiate treaties, although their acceptance requires approval of the Senate. The president is given the unconditional right to grant reprieves and pardons, except in cases of impeachment. The president is also given the power to appoint a variety of federal officials, including federal judges. These appointments must be approved by the Senate. The president is also the commander in chief of the nation's armed services.

Since the ratification of the Constitution, presidents have sought to expand their powers, especially in the realms of international affairs and war. Often, presidents avoid the constitutional treaty process by entering into executive agreements with other countries. Another area of increasing executive authority is the exercise of war powers. Presidents have used their powers as commander in chief to erode Congress's war powers. In recent decades, presidents have claimed that their duty to protect the nation may require them to send troops into battle without a formal congressional declaration of war. In 1973, Congress enacted the War Powers Act to impose a time limit on unilateral presidential use of military forces, but presidents have essentially ignored the Act and insisted that their duties required them to act decisively to protect the nation. Congress has generally acquiesced, though not without some protest, to use of presidential power in this area.

The Supreme Court has often supported the concentration of executive authority in foreign policy. *United States v. Curtiss-Wright Export Co.* (1936) has served as a basis for executive claims for exclusive authority over foreign policy. Often the Court will decline to referee in complaints against the president over foreign policy and war powers, citing separation of powers as the reason for judicial noninvolvement. (Under the "political questions" doctrine, the Court limits itself from hearing disputes that are committed to the other two branches.)

The Court has been more willing to examine and occasionally limit the use of executive "war powers" when that exercise impinges on individual rights, such as the right to trial or property ownership. Recently, in a number of cases arising from the Bush administration's Global War on Terror, the Supreme Court sought to set some limits on presidential actions. In 2004, the Supreme Court ruled that those labeled "enemy combatants" by the Bush administration and detained at Guantanamo Bay, Cuba, must be allowed to challenge their detention before a judge or neutral decision maker. The decision in *Hamdi v. Rumsfeld* rejected the administrative assertions of executive branch prerogative over determining the detention of citizens and noncitizens alike and stated memorably that "a state of war is not a blank check for the President." In 2006, the Court ruled in *Hamdan v. Rumsfeld* that the Bush administration's use of military tribunals to try terror suspects detained at Guantanamo Bay violated federal statutory and international law because the procedures to be used by the tribunals were not consistent with the Uniform Code of Military Justice and failed to observe key protections guaranteed by Common Article 3 of the Geneva Convention. Although the decision did not completely invalidate the use of tribunals, it required the administration and Congress to work together to provide an acceptable forum for these cases. In 2007, the Supreme Court ruled in *Boumediene v. Bush* that the alternate legal procedures established by the Military Commissions Act were an inadequate substitute for the judicial review protections of habeas corpus.

Section 3

[POWERS AND DUTIES OF THE PRESIDENT]
   He shall from time to time give to the Congress Information of the State of the Union, and recommend to their Consideration such Measures as he shall judge necessary and expedient; he may, on extraordinary Occasions, convene both Houses, or either of them, and in Case of Disagreement between them, with Respect to the Time of Adjournment, he may adjourn them to such Time as he shall think proper; he shall receive Ambassadors and other public Ministers; he shall take Care that the Laws be faithfully executed, and shall Commission all the Officers of the United States.

Presidents report to Congress every year on the state of the union. Section 3 requires only that the president "give to the Congress information of the state of the union, and recommend to their consideration such measures as he shall judge necessary and expedient." Although George Washington delivered his report to Congress as a formal address, Thomas Jefferson thought the address too kingly and chose instead to send a written report and agenda. Woodrow Wilson revived the practice of a formal speech to both houses of Congress in 1913. The advent of television has given the president the opportunity to use the State of the Union speech to appeal beyond Congress to the public at large.
   Congress also requires executive agencies to provide information on their activities. Presidents have asserted that they also have the power to withhold information

from Congress if the disclosure of such information would threaten the nation's security or the constitutional integrity of the executive branch. The latter claim is often called "**executive privilege**." In use since the days of George Washington, executive privilege has no textual underpinning in the Constitution but may be implicit in separation of powers and the president's role as commander in chief. The Supreme Court upheld the concept of executive privilege in the 1973 case of *United States v. Nixon*. Although President Nixon's claim of privilege in that particular case was denied, the Court found that presidents should receive great deference in matters of national security and defense, but that executive privilege claims were not without limit and must yield to the legitimate needs of the judicial process.

Section 4

[IMPEACHMENT]
   The President, Vice President and all civil Officers of the United States, shall be removed from Office on Impeachment for, and Conviction of, Treason, Bribery, or other high Crimes and Misdemeanors.

Presidents can be removed from office through the impeachment process. Two presidents, Andrew Johnson and Bill Clinton, have been impeached by the House, but neither was convicted by the Senate and both completed their terms. A recurring question in scholarly and popular debate about impeachment is what offenses constitute "high Crimes and Misdemeanors."

ARTICLE III

The framers of the Constitution thought it was important to create a federal judiciary even though every state already had a well-established system of courts. They feared that state courts would not give precedence to the interests of the federal government and would, instead, be prejudiced in favor of the states if conflicts arose between national and local interests.

No direct mention is made in the Constitution of judicial review—the power of courts to render the final decision when there is a conflict of interpretation of the Constitution or of federal laws between the courts and Congress, the courts and the executive branch, or the courts and the states. The Supreme Court assumed the power of judicial review through its early actions, particularly in the decisions of *Marbury v. Madison* (1803) and *Martin v. Hunter's Lessee* (1816).

Section 1

[JUDICIAL POWER, TENURE OF OFFICE]
   The judicial Power of the United States, shall be vested in one supreme Court, and in such inferior Courts as the Congress may from time to time ordain and establish. The Judges, both of the supreme and inferior Courts, shall hold their Offices during good

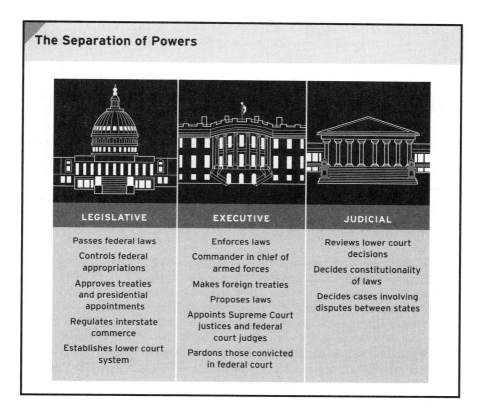

The Separation of Powers

LEGISLATIVE	EXECUTIVE	JUDICIAL
Passes federal laws	Enforces laws	Reviews lower court decisions
Controls federal appropriations	Commander in chief of armed forces	Decides constitutionality of laws
Approves treaties and presidential appointments	Makes foreign treaties	Decides cases involving disputes between states
Regulates interstate commerce	Proposes laws	
Establishes lower court system	Appoints Supreme Court justices and federal court judges	
	Pardons those convicted in federal court	

Behaviour, and shall, at stated Times, receive for their Services, a Compensation, which shall not be diminished during their Continuance in Office.

Section 1 of the judicial article establishes a Supreme Court and implies that Congress will subsequently create inferior courts. Federal judges and justices are appointed for life or "during good Behaviour," with the latter provision indicating that federal judges may be impeached and convicted by Congress. Since the ratification of the Constitution, Congress has established a comprehensive federal court system that includes district trial courts, regional courts of appeals, and specialized courts such as the Court of International Trade. Congress also determines the size of the Supreme Court, which has been set at nine since 1869, although President Franklin D. Roosevelt tried to have additional positions created on the Court in order to overcome judicial opposition to his New Deal programs.

Section 2

[JURISDICTION]
The judicial Power shall extend to all Cases, in Law and Equity, arising under this Constitution, the Laws of the United States, and Treaties made, or which shall be made,

under their Authority;—to all Cases affecting Ambassadors, other public Ministers and Consuls;—to all Cases of admiralty and maritime Jurisdiction;—to Controversies to which the United States shall be a Party;—to Controversies between two or more States;—*between a State and Citizens of another State;*—between Citizens of different States,—between Citizens of the same State claiming Lands under Grants of different States, *and between a State,* or the Citizens thereof, *and foreign States, Citizens or Subjects.*[11]

In all Cases affecting Ambassadors, other public Ministers and Consuls, and those in which a State shall be Party, the supreme Court shall have original Jurisdiction. In all the other Cases before mentioned, the supreme Court shall have appellate Jurisdiction, both as to Law and Fact, with such Exceptions, and under such Regulations as the Congress shall make.

The Trial of all Crimes, except in Cases of Impeachment, shall be by Jury; and such Trial shall be held in the State where the said Crimes shall have been committed; but when not committed within any State, the Trial shall be at such Place or Places as the Congress may by Law have directed.

Many of the types of cases likely to involve the interests of the federal government are declared to fall within the jurisdiction of the federal rather than the state courts. In particular, cases arising under the Constitution, cases under federal laws or treaties, and cases to which the federal government is a party are assigned to the federal courts. These jurisdictional rules are designed to ensure that cases in which the federal government has an important stake will be decided by federal judges. While the Constitution assigns the federal courts jurisdiction in certain types of cases, many other elements of federal court jurisdiction have been established by Congress via statute. From time to time, Congress modifies or restricts federal court jurisdiction in an effort to curb the power of the courts when legislators are dissatisfied with federal court rulings.

An important aspect of Article III, Section 2, is the assigning of judicial power to extend to all "cases and controversies." This stipulation means that there must be a real issue at stake—federal courts do not issue advisory opinions based on a hypothetical scenario. Individuals who bring a case before the federal court must have "standing to sue," articulated by Justice Brennan in *Baker v. Carr* (1962) as plaintiffs alleging "such a personal stake in the outcome of the controversy as to assure that concrete adverseness which sharpens the presentation of issues upon which the court so largely depends for illumination of difficult constitutional questions."

Section 3

[TREASON, PROOF, AND PUNISHMENT]

Treason against the United States, shall consist only in levying War against them, or in adhering to their Enemies, giving them Aid and Comfort. No Person shall be convicted

---

[11]Modified by Eleventh Amendment.

of Treason unless on the Testimony of two Witnesses to the same overt Act, or on Confession in open Court.

    The Congress shall have Power to declare the Punishment of Treason, but no Attainder of Treason shall work Corruption of Blood, or Forfeiture except during the Life of the Person attainted.

The Constitution defines the crime of treason and stipulates that individuals may not be held responsible for the treasonous conduct of family members. In Europe at the time, treason by one person might result in severe sanctions against an entire family.

ARTICLE IV

Article IV articulates the framers' concern with national unity and power. It includes provisions for comity (reciprocity) among states and among citizens of all states and for establishing the supremacy of the Constitution and national laws over those of the states.

Section 1

[FAITH AND CREDIT AMONG STATES]
    Full Faith and Credit shall be given in each State to the public Acts, Records, and judicial Proceedings of every other State. And the Congress may by general Laws prescribe the Manner in which such Acts, Records and Proceedings shall be proved, and the Effect thereof.

States are required to give "Full Faith and Credit" to the laws and acts of other states. This means that states must accept the contracts, public acts, and court documents of other states. Without this provision, known as comity, a driver's license or marriage license issued in one state would have no validity in a neighboring state. The full faith and credit clause has been largely uncontroversial. Recently, however, the prospect of some states legalizing same-sex marriage meant that other states could be required to honor those marriage licenses. In 1996, Congress passed, and President Clinton signed, the Defense of Marriage Act (DOMA), which specifies that "No state (or other political subdivision within the United States) need recognize a marriage between persons of the same sex, even if the marriage was concluded or recognized in another state." The act also states that the federal government is prohibited from recognizing same-sex or polygamous marriages for purposes such as income tax status. Critics charge that DOMA violates comity provisions, although DOMA supporters argue that federal action on this matter merely complies with the clause of Section 1 that allows for Congress to "prescribe the Manner in which such Acts, Records, and Proceedings shall be proved, and the Effect thereof." As of January 2011, five states (Massachusetts, Connecticut, Iowa, Vermont, and New

Hampshire) plus the District of Columbia allowed same-sex marriage. Thirty-one states had adopted laws blocking same-sex marriage. Gay rights legal groups are challenging the constitutionality of DOMA in several federal court cases. In February 2011, the Obama administration announced that the Justice Department no longer would defend DOMA against court challenges, leaving the status of the Act in limbo. In March 2011, the Republican leadership of the House of Representatives voted to intervene to defend DOMA in ongoing lawsuits. At the same time, some Democratic senators indicated their intention to introduce legislation to repeal DOMA.

Section 2

[PRIVILEGES AND IMMUNITIES, FUGITIVES]
   The Citizens of each State shall be entitled to all Privileges and Immunities of Citizens in the several States.
   A Person charged in any State with Treason, Felony or other Crime, who shall flee from Justice, and be found in another State, shall on Demand of the executive Authority of the State from which he fled, be delivered up, to be removed to the State having Jurisdiction of the Crime.
   No person held to Service or Labour in one State, under the Laws thereof, escaping into another, shall, in Consequence of any Law or Regulation therein, be discharged from such Service or Labour, but shall be delivered up on Claim of the Party to whom such Service or Labour may be due.[12]

States may not enact laws that promote policies that discriminate against citizens of other states. Over the decades, this provision has been applied mainly to prohibit state efforts to bar out-of-staters from access to natural resources. Many lesser forms of discrimination still exist. For example, every state charges out-of-staters a higher tuition than is paid by its own citizens if they wish to attend one of its publicly supported colleges or universities. States are also required to extradite or return fugitives from justice in other states.

Section 3

[ADMISSION OF NEW STATES]
   New States may be admitted by the Congress into this Union; but no new State shall be formed or erected within the Jurisdiction of any other State; nor any State be formed by the Junction of two or more States, or Parts of States, without the Consent of the Legislatures of the States concerned as well as of the Congress.
   The Congress shall have Power to dispose of and make all needful Rules and Regulations respecting the Territory or other Property belonging to the United States; and nothing

---

[12]Repealed by the Thirteenth Amendment.

in this Constitution shall be so construed as to Prejudice any Claims of the United States, or of any particular State.

Congress has the power to admit new states to the Union, but it may not do so by combining existing states or taking their territory without their permission. Congress directly governs all territory and possessions of the United States that are not part of a state.

Section 4

[GUARANTEE OF REPUBLICAN GOVERNMENT]
The United States shall guarantee to every State in this Union a Republican Form of Government, and shall protect each of them against Invasion; and on Application of the Legislature, or of the Executive (when the Legislature cannot be convened), against domestic Violence.

This section appears to mean that the federal government will intervene if a state adopts a form of government inconsistent with republican principles. Exactly how much popular participation is required by republican principles is an open matter. Thus far, no state has sought to establish a monarchy or dictatorship, but a challenge to a state constitution that disenfranchised a large part of the population came before the Court in the 1849 case of *Luther v. Borden.*

Luther was essentially a face-off between the representatives of two factions of Rhode Island society, both of which claimed to be the legitimate government for the state. The older government drew its legitimacy from the Royal Charter for the colony, which had, after the Revolution, become part of the state constitution. The constitution, however, disenfranchised a large part of the adult male population of the state based on property requirements. Another group called for a state constitutional convention, drafted a new document, and then called for a vote for a new government under the "revised" Constitution. Instead of choosing between the two potential governments, the Supreme Court said that it was up to the president and Congress, not the Court, to enforce this provision but declined to offer any opinion as to the circumstances that might warrant enforcement activities.

ARTICLE V

[AMENDMENT OF THE CONSTITUTION]
The Congress, whenever two thirds of both Houses shall deem it necessary, shall propose Amendments to this Constitution, or, on the Application of the Legislatures of two thirds of the several States, shall call a Convention for proposing Amendments, which, in either Case, shall be valid to all Intents and Purposes, as Part of this Constitution, when ratified by the Legislatures of three fourths of the several States, or by Conventions in three

Four Ways the Constitution Can Be Amended

*This method of proposal has never been employed. Thus amendment routes 3 and 4 have never been attempted.

†In each amendment proposal, Congress has the power to choose the method of ratification, the time limit for consideration by the states, and other conditions of ratification. The movement to repeal Prohibition in the Twenty-First Amendment was the only occasion in which route 2 was used successfully. See Richard B. Bernstein, *Amending America: If We Love the Constitution So Much, Why Do We Keep Trying to Change It?* (Lawrence: University of Kansas Press, 1993), esp. pp. 176–77.

The National Level: Proposal of Amendments

A Passage in House and Senate, each by two-thirds vote

B* Passage in a national convention called by Congress in response to petitions by two-thirds of the states (34 states)

Route 1, Route 2, Route 3, Route 4

The State Level: Ratification of Amendments

C† Acceptance by majority vote in the legislatures of three-fourths of the states (38 states)

D† Acceptance by conventions called for the purpose, in three-fourths of the states (38 states)

fourths thereof, as the one or the other Mode of Ratification may be proposed by the Congress; *Provided that no Amendment which may be made prior to the Year One thousand eight hundred and eight shall in any Manner affect the first and fourth Clauses in the Ninth Section of the first Article;*[13] and that no State, without its Consent, shall be deprived of its equal Suffrage in the Senate.

Recall that the original purpose of the Constitutional Convention was to amend the Articles of Confederation. A major drawback of the Articles of Confederation was that it required unanimous consent for any amendment to the national power. Unanimity proved unworkable. Therefore, the framers sought to create a constitution that could be amended more easily than the Articles, but remain insulated from sudden shifts in public opinion.

The Constitution may be amended if two-thirds of the state legislatures or two-thirds of both houses of Congress propose a change and three-fourths of the states then ratify the proposal. States may ratify a proposed amendment by a vote of their legislatures or by calling a special convention. Article V does not mention the possibility that the Constitution could be amended or even rewritten by a new national constitutional convention modeled on the 1787 meeting. Some scholars believe that

[13]Temporary provision.

such a convention could be called, while others assert that the absence of a constitutional provision for such a conclave means that it could not legally be organized.

Since the Constitution's adoption, only twenty-seven amendments have been added to the original text. The first ten, known as the Bill of Rights, were added in 1791 as a concession to Antifederalist opposition to the new Constitution. Thus, since the time of the Constitution's framing, the Constitution has really been amended only seventeen more times. The successful amendments primarily have been concerned with the structure or composition of government. Many amendments have been proposed in Congress, but few survive the rigorous ratification process. The Equal Rights Amendment (ERA), which would have added a constitutional guarantee of equal rights based on sex, was one of the very few proposals that got the necessary two-thirds vote in Congress, but failed to obtain enough state ratifications. The ERA fell only three states short of ratification.

ARTICLE VI

[DEBTS, SUPREMACY, OATH]

All Debts contracted and Engagements entered into, before the Adoption of this Constitution, shall be as valid against the United States under this Constitution, as under the Confederation.

This Constitution, and the Laws of the United States which shall be made in Pursuance thereof; and all Treaties made, or which shall be made, under the Authority of the United States, shall be the supreme Law of the Land; and the Judges in every State shall be bound thereby, any Thing in the Constitution or Laws of any State to the Contrary notwithstanding.

The Senators and Representatives before mentioned, and the Members of the several State Legislatures, and all executive and judicial Officers, both of the United States and of the several States, shall be bound by Oath or Affirmation, to support this Constitution; but no religious Test shall be required as a Qualification to any Office or public Trust under the United States.

The most important element of Article VI is the second paragraph declaring the Constitution and federal law to be the supreme law of the land. This paragraph established the principle of federal supremacy and, in effect, asserted that the United States was one nation bound by one body of law. The notion of federal legal supremacy has occasionally been challenged. In the 1830s, John C. Calhoun of South Carolina promoted a doctrine he called "nullification." This was the idea that if a state found a federal law to be objectionable or unconstitutional, it could declare the law to be null and void within its own borders. South Carolina's legislature voted to nullify a federal tariff but retreated in the face of threats from President Andrew Jackson. This incident did not settle challenges to federal supremacy. In the 1958 case of *Cooper v. Aaron*, the Supreme Court unanimously rejected Arkansas's assertion that the state was not required to obey the Supreme Court's school desegregation rulings.

ARTICLE VII

[RATIFICATION AND ESTABLISHMENT]
The Ratification of the Conventions of nine States, shall be sufficient for the Establishment of this Constitution between the States so ratifying the Same.[14]

Done in Convention by the Unanimous Consent of the States present the Seventeenth Day of September in the Year of our Lord one thousand seven hundred and Eighty seven and of the Independence of the United States of America the Twelfth. *In Witness* whereof We have hereunto subscribed our Names,

The framers were concerned that not all the states would ratify the Constitution; hence they stipulated that the Constitution would take effect after nine states agreed to it.

Federalists versus Antifederalists

	FEDERALISTS	ANTIFEDERALISTS
Who were they?	Property owners, creditors, merchants	Small farmers, frontiersmen, debtors, shopkeepers
What did they believe?	Believed that elites were best fit to govern; feared "excessive democracy"	Believed that government should be closer to the people; feared concentration of power in hands of the elites
What system of government did they favor?	Favored strong national government; believed in "filtration" so that only elites would obtain governmental power	Favored retention of power by state governments and protection of individual rights
Who were their leaders?	Alexander Hamilton, James Madison, George Washington	Patrick Henry, George Mason, Elbridge Gerry, George Clinton

[14]The Constitution was submitted on September 17, 1787, by the Constitutional Convention, was ratified by the conventions of several states at various dates up to May 29, 1790, and became effective on March 4, 1789.

Indeed, they had reason to be concerned—the struggle for ratification by the thirteen colonies had to be carried out in thirteen separate political contexts, influenced by both national and local considerations. Generally, two camps faced off over ratification, the Federalists and the Antifederalists. Ultimately, the Federalists would prevail, but not without some important concessions to the Antifederalists (see Table "Federalists versus Antifederalists"). On June 21, 1788, New Hampshire became the ninth state to ratify the Constitution. Virginia and New York followed shortly thereafter. It would be over another year before North Carolina and Rhode Island, the last of the original colonies, would ratify the Constitution.

The Bill of Rights

The first ten amendments to the Constitution are commonly known as the Bill of Rights. Antifederalists (who had not been delegates to the Constitutional Convention) picked up the argument of Thomas Jefferson (who also had not been a delegate to the Convention) that a major defect of the new constitution was its omission of a bill of rights.

Rights in the Original Constitution (Not in the Bill of Rights)	
CLAUSE	RIGHT ESTABLISHED
Article I, Sec. 9	guarantee of habeas corpus
Article I, Sec. 9	prohibition of **bills of attainder**
Article I, Sec. 9	prohibition of **ex post facto laws**
Article I, Sec. 9	prohibition against acceptance of titles of nobility, etc., from any foreign state
Article III	guarantee of trial by jury in state where crime was committed
Article III	treason defined and limited to the life of the person convicted, not to the person's heirs

Federalists argued that a bill of rights was unnecessary in a government of limited, enumerated powers, and, further, that such a bill might be dangerously limiting. Distrustful of central government's willingness to abide by those limitations, Antifederalists argued that a bill of rights was necessary to protect individuals from unwarranted governmental intrusion into their lives. The promise to adopt a bill of rights was critical to the ratification of the Constitution by key states such as Massachusetts, Virginia, New York, and Maryland.

James Madison, having been elected to the new Congress to represent his home state of Virginia, quickly introduced amendments to the Constitution as one of the first orders of business of the House of Representatives. The House of Representatives ultimately adopted seventeen amendments; of these, the Senate adopted twelve. Ten of those would be ratified by the states in 1791. (One of the original twelve amendments, one that did not achieve inclusion in the Bill of Rights, the provision on congressional pay increases, would ultimately be ratified in 1992 and become the Twenty-Seventh Amendment.)

The Bill of Rights was clearly intended to set limits for the federal government, but did its protections of individual liberties also apply to the state governments? In *Barron v. Baltimore* (1833), the Supreme Court held that the Bill of Rights was

The Bill of Rights

Amendment I: Limits on Congress
Congress cannot make any law establishing a religion or abridging freedoms of religious exercise, speech, assembly, or petition.

Amendments II, III, IV: Limits on the Executive
The executive branch cannot infringe on the right of the people to keep arms (II), cannot arbitrarily take houses for militia (III), and cannot search for or seize evidence without a court warrant swearing to the probable existence of a crime (IV).

Amendments V, VI, VII, VIII: Limits on the Judiciary
The courts cannot hold trials for serious offenses without provision for a grand jury (V), a trial jury (VII), a speedy trial (VI), presentation of charges and confrontation by the accused of hostile witnesses (VI), and immunity from testimony against oneself and immunity from trial more than once for the same offense (V). Furthermore, neither bail nor punishment can be excessive (VIII), and no property can be taken without "just compensation" (V).

Amendments IX, X: Limits on the National Government
Any rights not enumerated are reserved to the state or the people (X), but the enumeration of certain rights in the Constitution should not be interpreted to mean that those are the only rights the people have (IX).

Incorporation of the Bill of Rights into the Fourteenth Amendment

SELECTED PROVISIONS AND AMENDMENTS	NOT INCORPORATED UNTIL	KEY CASE
Eminent domain (V)	1897	*Chicago, Burlington, and Quincy R.R. v. Chicago*
Freedom of speech (I)	1925	*Gitlow v. New York*
Freedom of press (I)	1931	*Near v. Minnesota*
Free exercise of religion (I)	1934	*Hamilton v. Regents of the University of California*
Freedom of assembly (I) and freedom to petition the government for redress of grievances (I)	1937	*DeJonge v. Oregon*
Freedom of assembly (I)	1939	*Hague v. CIO*
Nonestablishment of state religion (I)	1947	*Emerson v. Board of Education*
Freedom from unnecessary search and seizure (IV)	1949	*Wolf v. Colorado*
Freedom from warrantless search and seizure (IV) ("exclusionary rule")	1961	*Mapp v. Ohio*
Freedom from cruel and unusual punishment (VIII)	1962	*Robinson v. California*
Right to counsel in any criminal trial (VI)	1963	*Gideon v. Wainwright*
Right against self-incrimination and forced confessions (V)	1964	*Mallory v. Hogan Escobedo v. Illinois*
Right to counsel and remain silent (V)	1966	*Miranda v. Arizona*
Right against double jeopardy (V)	1969	*Benton v. Maryland*
Right to bear arms (II)	2010	*McDonald v. Chicago*

intended to apply only to the federal government. It was only through the addition to the Constitution and interpretation of the Fourteenth Amendment that the Supreme Court would begin to selectively incorporate the provisions of the Bill of Rights against the states.

AMENDMENT I

[FREEDOM OF RELIGION, OF SPEECH, AND OF THE PRESS]
Congress shall make no law respecting an establishment of religion, or prohibiting the free exercise thereof; or abridging the freedom of speech, or of the press; or the right of the people peaceably to assemble, and to petition the Government for a redress of grievances.

The First Amendment guarantees freedom of speech, religion, press, assembly, and the right to petition the government. Most Americans view these protections as fundamental to a free society.

While the First Amendment seems to be written in absolute terms, asserting that Congress "shall make no law," the reality is a bit different. Congress and the states make many laws that restrict speech and the other freedoms in service of protecting

The Protection of Free Speech by the First Amendment

	PROTECTED SPEECH	UNPROTECTED SPEECH
If content is true:	All speech is protected by the First Amendment when it is the truth.	"True" speech can be regulated *only*: • If it fails the "clear and present danger" test, or • If it falls below community standards of obscenity or pornography.
If content is false:	Defamatory speech is protected when: • Spoken or written by a public official in the course of official business, or • Spoken or written by a citizen or the press against people in the public eye.	"False" speech can be regulated or punished *only* when it can be demonstrated that there was a reckless disregard for the truth (as in libel or slander).

the public health, safety, and welfare. Courts attempt to balance the need for community protection against individuals' rights. In *Brandenburg v. Ohio* (1969), the Supreme Court held that government may only restrict speech that is likely to incite imminent unlawful action. Government may not restrict speech based on its content (with narrow exceptions for obscenity and "fighting words"), but may impose restrictions on the time, place, or manner in which speech is conducted. Thus, a city cannot forbid speeches against its school funding plan, for example, but may require that any speech maker apply for a permit to address a crowd in front of school department headquarters. The First Amendment also protects symbolic speech, in which political views are expressed through images and action, but not necessarily through words. Examples of this include the burning of an American flag (*Texas v. Johnson* [1989]) or the wearing of a black armband to protest war (*Tinker v. Des Moines* [1969]).

Recent First Amendment controversy has concerned the regulation of campaign finances. The Bipartisan Campaign Reform Act of 2002, also known as McCain-Feingold, banned the "electioneering communications" paid for by corporations or labor unions from their general funds in the thirty days before a presidential primary and in the sixty days before the general elections. In 2008, the conservative group Citizens United was prevented from airing *Hillary: The Movie* and advertisements for the film on television during the 2008 presidential primaries. In 2010, a closely divided Supreme Court ruled in *Citizens United v. Federal Election Commission* that the government may not ban independent political spending by corporations in candidate elections because this regulation violates the principle that government should not regulate political speech. Supporters of the decision argued that it prevented government interference with the First Amendment, while critics, including President Obama in his 2010 State of the Union address, argued that the decision would allow corporate and special interests overwhelming influence in elections.

Some speech is not protected at all. If a written statement is made in "reckless disregard of the truth" and is considered damaging to the victim because it is "malicious, scandalous, and defamatory," it can be punished as libel. If an oral statement of such nature is made, it can be punished as slander. Obscenity falls outside of the area of protected speech, but the courts have had a difficult time creating clear guidelines for what materials are considered obscene. In recent years, the battle against obscene speech has been against "cyberporn"—pornography on the Internet. The Supreme Court has struck down efforts by Congress to regulate adults' online access to explicit materials, but has upheld measures that seek to limit children's access to pornography, such as requiring antipornography filters on public library computers, and those measures that criminalize the online transmission of child pornography.

Closely related to speech in terms of its necessity to democratic society is freedom of the press. The press in the United States enjoys a wide range of latitude to print or air whatever information it sees fit. Press establishments may be sued for libel, but in *New York Times Co. v. Sullivan* (1964), the Supreme Court narrowed the protection that libel suits give public officials. In order for public officials to prevail in a libel suit, they must prove that the media institution knowingly or recklessly published false information.

The First Amendment also prohibits the government from establishing a religion. The framers meant that the government was barred from declaring one particular religion to be the nation's official faith, as was then the case in England and other countries. In recent years, the Supreme Court has held that the **establishment clause** prohibits many forms of government support for religion as well as many forms of religious exercise in public institutions such as schools.

Governments must adopt a similarly neutral stance toward the **free exercise** of religion. Any government action that affects how an individual exercises his or her religion must meet the highest judicial test of **strict scrutiny**. The action must have a compelling state interest and be carried out by the least restrictive means available.

AMENDMENT II

[RIGHT TO KEEP AND BEAR ARMS]
A well regulated Militia, being necessary to the security of a free State, the right of the people to keep and bear Arms, shall not be infringed.

The point of the Second Amendment is the provision for militias as police and military resources for state and local governments. Some Americans see the Second Amendment's outlining of a right to bear arms as an individual freedom as well. In 2008, the Supreme Court declared in *District of Columbia v. Heller* that the Second Amendment protected an individual's right to possess a firearm for private use and struck down a District of Columbia law that made it very difficult for individuals to purchase private firearms. Because the District of Columbia is an entity of the federal government, the Second Amendment was not applied to the states until the 2010 case of *McDonald v. Chicago*, when the Supreme Court struck down a Chicago firearms ordinance. This case repeated the Supreme Court's explanation of the Second Amendment as protecting an individual right and was the first new incorporation decision by the Court in forty years.

AMENDMENT III

[QUARTERING OF SOLDIERS]
No Soldier shall, in time of peace be quartered in any house, without the consent of the Owner, nor in time of war, but in a manner to be prescribed by law.

Under British law, individuals could be compelled to house soldiers at their own expense. The Constitution prohibits this practice. This matter was of great concern at the time of the Founding, but largely is an ignored provision today.

AMENDMENT IV

[SECURITY FROM UNWARRANTABLE SEARCH AND SEIZURE]
   The right of the people to be secure in their persons, houses, papers, and effects, against unreasonable searches and seizures, shall not be violated, and no Warrants shall issue, but upon probable cause, supported by Oath or affirmation, and particularly describing the place to be searched, and the persons or things to be seized.

The Fourth Amendment prohibits "unreasonable" searches and seizures, a category that includes arrests, wiretapping, and electronic surveillance. The basic standard for what constitutes reasonableness is probable cause and a particularized warrant issued by a neutral magistrate. The purpose of the Fourth Amendment is to protect privacy. Thus, its protections are strongest where both subjective and objective expectations of privacy exist, such as in a person's home. Before the police can search an individual's home, in most cases they must obtain a warrant from a judge after presenting evidence to justify their intrusion.

   The rules governing searches are complex and also somewhat flexible. The applicability of the Fourth Amendment to a particular situation will call into consideration concepts of the "level of intrusiveness and coerciveness of the search," "legitimate expectations of privacy," and "reasonableness of the search in the situation." In the 1961 case of *Mapp v. Ohio* the Supreme Court established the **exclusionary rule** that prohibited prosecutors from using all evidence obtained directly or indirectly as a result of an improper search. It was also in the *Mapp* case that the Supreme Court held that the freedom from warrantless search and seizure applied to the states as well as the federal government. In recent years, though, the federal courts have allowed a variety of warrantless searches if the search meets a recognized exception criterion, among which are situations in which an individual consents to the search, items are displayed in plain sight, or reasonable suspicion exists that a crime has been or is about to be committed (*Terry v. Ohio* [1968]). In 2009, the Supreme Court held that judges should exclude evidence only when police behavior was "deliberate, reckless or grossly negligent" (*Herring v. United States*).

   As technology advances, the potential for the state to use technology in surveillance is also growing. In the case of *Kyollo v. United States* (2001), the Court was asked to determine whether a thermal imaging scan (conducted from the outside) of an individual's home (to search for "hot spots" that could be consistent with heating lamps used in growing marijuana plants) violated the Fourth Amendment. The Court held that when "the Government uses a device that is not in general public use, to explore details of a private home that would previously have been unknowable without physical intrusion," the surveillance counts as a Fourth Amendment search and requires a warrant.

AMENDMENT V

[RIGHTS OF ACCUSED PERSONS IN CRIMINAL PROCEEDINGS]

No person shall be held to answer for a capital, or otherwise infamous crime, unless on a presentment or indictment of a Grand Jury, except in cases arising in the land or naval forces, or in the Militia, when in actual service in time of War or in public danger; nor shall any person be subject for the same offence to be twice put in jeopardy of life or limb; nor shall be compelled in any criminal case to be a witness against himself, nor be deprived of life, liberty, or property, without due process of law; nor shall private property be taken for public use, without just compensation.

The Fifth Amendment contains a number of provisions protecting individuals from arbitrary government action. Persons accused of serious crimes cannot be brought to trial unless the evidence against them is presented to a grand jury consisting of ordinary citizens. This provision is designed to prevent the government from prosecuting individuals on the basis of secret evidence. Once an individual is acquitted of a crime, he or she cannot be prosecuted again. Trying a defendant more than once for the same crime is called **double jeopardy** and could be used by the government to exhaust the resources of a defendant.

Most Americans are familiar with the part of the Fifth Amendment that provides protections against self-incrimination, a protection that is often referred to as "taking the Fifth." Defendants cannot be compelled to testify against themselves. This provision is designed to prevent coerced confessions. In the 1966 case of *Miranda v. Arizona*, the Supreme Court held that this provision meant that individuals had the right to refuse to speak when being questioned by the police. One need only turn on the television to see the familiar *Miranda* warnings being read to suspects under arrest. Many in Congress and law enforcement were quite critical of *Miranda* when it was announced because they believed it would interfere with police work and obstruct public safety. As the Supreme Court has interpreted *Miranda* over the years, it has recognized a number of exceptions and situations in which questioning may take place without the warnings being read. In *Dickerson v. United States* (2000), the Court was asked to determine the constitutionality of a federal statute enacted immediately after the *Miranda* decision that attempted to overrule the decision. Chief Justice William Rehnquist started his announcement of the Court's decision to uphold *Miranda* with the familiar formulation of "You have the right to remain silent. . . ." In *Dickerson,* the Court upheld self-incrimination and coerced confession rules as they had developed from *Miranda* and in subsequent decisions that limited or carved out exceptions to *Miranda*. In 2010, the Supreme Court introduced an important qualification to the *Miranda* rule. In *Berghuis v. Thomkins*, the Supreme Court said that statements made by suspects who did not expressly waive their rights (usually by signing a form) could be used against them at trial.

The Fifth Amendment also stipulates that individuals cannot be fined or incarcerated arbitrarily, but are entitled to a proper legal process.

Finally, the takings clause of the Fifth Amendment limits the power of **eminent domain,** the government's power to seize private property for a public use. The Fifth Amendment requires the government to compensate the property owner for the just value of the land or other property that is to be seized. Additionally, local, state, and federal restrictions on the use of land that do not seize it outright but do affect its value or use are considered "regulatory takings" that are also subject to constitutional review. In *Dolan v. City of Tigard* (1994), the Court held that restrictions on the use of private land must serve a legitimate governmental objective and show a "rough proportionality" to the objective. However, the recent case of *Kelo v. City of New London* (2005) gives broad latitude to governments to define the "public purposes" for which land may be taken. In this case, the Court upheld New London's use of eminent domain to take property that would be used by a private developer for a large commercial development and compelled the neighborhood

The Rights of the Accused from Arrest to Trial

No improper searches and seizures (Fourth Amendment)
No arrest without probable cause (Fourth Amendment)
Right to remain silent (Fifth Amendment)
No self-incrimination during arrest or trial (Fifth Amendment)
Right to be informed of charges (Sixth Amendment)
Right to counsel (Sixth Amendment)
No excessive bail (Eighth Amendment)
Right to grand jury (Fifth Amendment)
Right to open trial before a judge (Article I, Section 9)
Right to speedy and public trial before an impartial jury (Sixth Amendment)
Evidence obtained by illegal search not admissible during trial (Fourth Amendment)
Right to confront witnesses (Sixth Amendment)
No double jeopardy (Fifth Amendment)
No cruel and unusual punishment (Eighth Amendment)

homeowners to accept compensation from the city. Many conservative and libertarian groups strongly opposed the Court's ruling in *Kelo*. Some expressed their dismay by trying (unsuccessfully) to convince local governments to use their power of eminent domain to take and develop vacation property owned by justices who had signed the majority opinion in *Kelo*. Others were more successful in getting state legislatures to amend their *state* constitutions to limit state and local government eminent domain powers.

AMENDMENT VI

[RIGHT TO SPEEDY TRIAL, WITNESSES, ETC.]
In all criminal prosecutions, the accused shall enjoy the right to a speedy and public trial, by an impartial jury of the State and district wherein the crime shall have been committed, which district shall have been previously ascertained by law, and to be informed of the nature and cause of the accusation; to be confronted with the witnesses against him; to have compulsory process for obtaining witnesses in his favor, and to have the Assistance of Counsel for his defence.

In eighteenth-century Europe individuals believed by the government to be guilty of an offense could be held for many years without being charged, eventually tried in secret before a government tribunal, not allowed to question witnesses, and deprived of legal assistance. The Sixth Amendment is an effort to ensure that criminal defendants in the United States will have the right to speedy public trials before local juries, that they will be represented by counsel, and that they will be able to confront their accusers, see the evidence against them, and bring their own witnesses to testify on their behalf. Since its ratification in 1791, the Sixth Amendment has protected individuals from the actions of the federal government. But it was not until a series of Supreme Court decisions in the 1960s that the Sixth Amendment also applied to state action. One of the most notable of these decisions was *Gideon v. Wainwright* (1963), which applied the right to counsel to state defendants. In 2009, the Supreme Court said in *Melendez-Diaz v. Massachusetts* that criminal defendants have the right to cross-examine crime lab analysts and, if defendants are not given that opportunity, the crime lab reports prepared by those analysts cannot be used at trial.

AMENDMENT VII

[TRIAL BY JURY IN CIVIL CASES]
In suits at common law, where the value in controversy shall exceed twenty dollars, the right of trial by jury shall be preserved, and no fact tried by a jury, shall be otherwise reexamined in any Court of the United States, than according to the rules of the common law.

Defendants in federal civil suits are entitled to jury trials if the amount at stake is significant. By statute, the amount is now $75,000 rather than the $20 stipulated in the Constitution. The Seventh Amendment has not been applied to the states, which are free to set their own rules.

AMENDMENT VIII

[BAILS, FINES, PUNISHMENTS]
Excessive bail shall not be required, nor excessive fines imposed, nor cruel and unusual punishments inflicted.

Individuals accused of committing crimes are presumed innocent until proven guilty in court. If such individuals believe that they are likely to be found guilty, they may flee to avoid trial. However, if they are incarcerated to prevent flight, the presumption of innocence is being violated through the jailing of innocent persons. Bail, a monetary bond that will be forfeited if the defendant does not appear for trial, is an instrument designed to guarantee that a defendant will not flee while allowing technically innocent persons to remain free while awaiting trial. The Seventh Amendment stipulates that excessive bail should not be required but offers no guidance as to what might be considered excessive. The Supreme Court, however, has held that when setting bail judges should take into account such factors as the severity of the crime with which defendants have been charged, the danger they may represent to the community, and the risk that they will attempt to flee. In *United States v. Salerno* (1987), the Court upheld a federal statute that allowed the government to hold defendants in federal trials without bail prior to trial provided the government could prove that no release conditions could reasonably ensure public safety.

The courts have interpreted "cruel and unusual" punishment to mean that most forms of corporal punishment, such as flogging or branding (both common in the eighteenth century), were prohibited. The Supreme Court has also asserted that the Eighth Amendment requires a measure of proportionality between the crime and the punishment. In the 1983 case of *Solem v. Helm*, the Court said that punishment must not be excessive in relation to the crime committed.

Perhaps the debate most associated with the interpretation of "cruel and unusual" is the debate over the constitutionality of the death penalty. Many Americans believe that the death penalty is a form of cruel and unusual punishment. Others argue that the death penalty was certainly contemplated by the framers and that it has a deterrent effect today. The Supreme Court, however, has never said that the death penalty per se is unconstitutional, although it did halt executions nationwide in 1972 with its decision in *Furman v. Georgia*. In *Furman*, the Court invalidated death sentences without statutory guidelines for the arbitrary and discriminatory manner in which they were applied. Blacks were more likely than whites to be sentenced to death; poor people more likely than rich ones; and men more often than women. Executions resumed after *Gregg v. Georgia* (1976) upheld statutory guidelines and a bifurcated trial process in which guilt/innocence and sentencing were handled in two separate jury phases. The Supreme Court has ruled that the death penalty constitutes cruel and unusual punishment for mentally retarded criminals (*Atkins v. Virginia* [2002]) and those who were minors when they committed their crime (*Roper v. Simmons* [2005]). In 2010, the Supreme Court said in *Graham v. Florida* that life sentences without chance of parole for juveniles who have not committed murder also constitute cruel and unusual punishment. Renewed attention was drawn to the debate over the death penalty after Justice John Paul Stevens retired from the Supreme Court in 2010 and gave extensive public criticism of the death penalty.

AMENDMENT IX

[RESERVATION OF RIGHTS OF PEOPLE]
   The enumeration in the Constitution, of certain rights, shall not be construed to deny or disparage others retained by the people.

The Bill of Rights is not an exhaustive list of the rights of Americans. The omission of a right does not mean that it does not exist. The courts and the Congress may identify other rights to which Americans are entitled. For example, in *Griswold v. Connecticut* (1965) and *Roe v. Wade* (1973) the Supreme Court said that Americans were entitled to a right of privacy. In *Lawrence v. Texas* (2003), the Supreme Court extended the right of privacy to homosexuals with a dramatic pronouncement that gays are "entitled to respect for their private lives" as a matter of constitutional due process. State legislatures no longer had the authority to make private consensual sexual behavior a crime. The right to privacy may also encompass a right to die. Although the Supreme Court has not ruled definitely on the issue, in 2006 it upheld a Washington state law that allowed doctors to use drugs to facilitate the deaths of terminally ill patients who requested such assistance.

   From time to time, Congress has established rights by statute. For example, federal legislation has given individuals with disabilities the right to reasonable workplace accommodation.

AMENDMENT X

[POWERS RESERVED TO STATES OR PEOPLE]
   The powers not delegated to the United States by the Constitution, nor prohibited by it to the States, are reserved to the States respectively, or to the people.

Opponents of the Constitution argued that the framers intended to create a national government that would destroy the autonomy of the states. The Tenth Amendment was designed to allay these fears by asserting that the national government would exercise only those powers specifically granted to it by the Constitution. For much of the twentieth century, Congress's powers under the commerce clause were so strong that the Tenth Amendment did not serve as a check on federal power. In the 1941 case of *United States v. Darby,* the Supreme Court dismissed the Tenth Amendment as a "truism."

During the 1990s, however, the Supreme Court struck down several federal statutes as exceeding the government's constitutional powers. These cases form what is sometimes referred to as the Rehnquist Court's "federalism revival." In *New York v. United States* (1992), *United States v. Lopez* (1995), *Printz v. United States* (1997), and *United States v. Morrison* (2000), the Court limited Congress's power under the commerce clause, sometimes explicitly using the Tenth Amendment and other times referring to principles of federalism more broadly.

Other Amendments

AMENDMENT XI

[Proposed by Congress on March 4, 1794; declared ratified on January 8, 1798.]
[RESTRICTION OF JUDICIAL POWER]
 The Judicial power of the United States shall not be construed to extend to any suit in law or equity, commenced or prosecuted against one of the United States by Citizens of another State, or by Citizens or Subjects of any Foreign State.

In the 1792 case of *Chisholm v. Georgia*, the Supreme Court ruled that individuals could sue states in federal court and that states did not enjoy sovereign immunity from suits filed by citizens of other states. Sovereign immunity is the idea that governments cannot be sued unless they consent. An outcry from the state legislatures resulted in the Eleventh Amendment, which affirmed the states' sovereign immunity. While the Eleventh Amendment refers only to suits brought against states by noncitizens, the Supreme Court held in the 1890 case of *Hans v. Louisiana* that the amendment established a broad principle of sovereign immunity. This immunity is not absolute and may be limited by Congress pursuant to its own exercise of constitutional powers. However, in the 1990s, in conjunction with the Rehnquist Court's federalism cases under the Tenth Amendment, the Eleventh Amendment also served as a resource for a reassertion of state sovereignty and a check on Congress's powers under the commerce clause (*Seminole Tribe of Florida v. Florida* [1996], *Alden v. Maine* [1999], and *Kimel v. Florida Board of Regents* [2000]).

AMENDMENT XII

[*Proposed by Congress on December 9, 1803; declared ratified on September 25, 1804.*]

[ELECTION OF PRESIDENT AND VICE PRESIDENT]

The Electors shall meet in their respective states and vote by ballot for President and Vice-President, one of whom, at least, shall not be an inhabitant of the same state with themselves; they shall name in their ballots the person voted for as President, and in distinct ballots the person voted for as Vice-President, and they shall make distinct lists of all persons voted for as President, and of all persons voted for as Vice-President, and of the number of votes for each, which lists they shall sign and certify, and transmit sealed to the seat of the government of the United States, directed to the President of the Senate;—the President of the Senate shall, in presence of the Senate and House of Representatives, open all the certificates and the votes shall then be counted;—The person having the greatest number of votes for President, shall be the President, if such number be a majority of the whole number of Electors appointed; and if no person have such majority, then from the persons having the highest numbers not exceeding three on the list of those voted for as President, the House of Representatives shall choose immediately, by ballot, the President. But in choosing the President, the votes shall be taken by states, the representation from each state having one vote; a quorum for this purpose shall consist of a member or members from two-thirds of the states, and a majority of all the states shall be necessary to a choice. And if the House of Representatives shall not choose a President whenever the right of choice shall devolve upon them, before the fourth day of March next following, then the Vice-President shall act as President, as in the case of the death or other constitutional disability of the President.—The person having the greatest number of votes as Vice-President, shall be the Vice-President, if such number be a majority of the whole number of Electors appointed, and if no person have a majority, then from the two highest numbers on the list, the Senate shall choose the Vice-President; a quorum for the purpose shall consist of two-thirds of the whole number of Senators, and a majority of the whole number shall be necessary to a choice. But no person constitutionally ineligible to the office of President shall be eligible to that of Vice-President of the United States.

The 1800 presidential election caused a crisis in the fledgling republic. Thomas Jefferson was the presidential candidate of the Democratic-Republican party, and Aaron Burr was the party's vice-presidential candidate. However, the electoral procedures established by Article II did not distinguish between presidential and vice presidential votes, and each of the men received seventy-three electoral votes. Until Alexander Hamilton, leader of the Federalist party, put a stop to it, some Federalist electors considered casting their votes for Burr to thwart their hated rival, Jefferson. The Twelfth Amendment requires electors to vote separately for president and vice president.

AMENDMENT XIII

[Proposed by Congress on January 31, 1865; declared ratified on December 18, 1865.]

Section 1

[ABOLITION OF SLAVERY]
Neither slavery nor involuntary servitude, except as a punishment for crime whereof the party shall have been duly convicted, shall exist within the United States, or any place subject to their jurisdiction.

Section 2

[POWER TO ENFORCE THIS ARTICLE]
Congress shall have power to enforce this article by appropriate legislation.

With the victory of the Union army all but certain, Congress moved to abolish slavery by constitutional amendment. In the *Civil Rights Cases* (1883), the Supreme Court seemed to indicate that the Thirteenth Amendment prohibited not only the practice of slavery, but also its "badges and incidents." Yet in the same case the Court held that Congress had no power to prohibit racial discrimination in public accommodation. The modern Civil Rights Movement would focus most of its attention on achieving a legal framework for equality through the Fourteenth Amendment.

AMENDMENT XIV

Section 1

[Proposed by Congress on June 13, 1866; declared ratified on July 28, 1868.]
[CITIZENSHIP RIGHTS NOT TO BE ABRIDGED BY STATES]
All persons born or naturalized in the United States, and subject to the jurisdiction thereof, are citizens of the United States and of the State wherein they reside. No State shall make or enforce any law which shall abridge the privileges or immunities of citizens of the United States; nor shall any State deprive any person of life, liberty, or property, without due process of law; nor deny to any person within its jurisdiction the equal protection of the laws.

Section 1 of the Fourteenth Amendment nationalizes American citizenship and prohibits the states from depriving citizens of rights to which they would be entitled by the federal Constitution, including "due process of law" and "the **equal protection** of the laws." It is on the basis of the Fourteenth Amendment that the Supreme Court has gradually held that the states may not undertake actions inconsistent with the federal Bill of Rights. For this reason, Section 1 of the Fourteenth Amendment is generally seen as one of the most important constitutional amendments.

The Fourteenth Amendment gives little guidance on what constitutes equal protection of the laws. For much of American history, large portions of the population were not considered part of "We the People." The Fourteenth Amendment has been read in the twentieth and twenty-first centuries to change that, directing judicial scrutiny to the treatment of "discrete and insular minorities" (*United States v. Carolene Products* [1938]).

The development of equal protection law in the United States has been central to efforts to eliminate racial, gender, and other forms of discrimination. The equal protection clause does not create substantive rights per se as much as it measures the validity of classifications made in law and their effect on individuals. The equal protection clause applies to all persons, not just citizens of the United States, and has been interpreted to prohibit discrimination in formal laws, rules, and policies, and also to prohibit intentional discrimination in the administration or enforcement of a law that is neutral on its face. The equal protection clause does not prevent all forms of discrimination, but rather those that are state action (action by a state, county, local, or otherwise public official). Private discriminatory action must be linked to state action in order for it to violate the equal protection clause (*Shelley v. Kraemer* [1948], *Moose Lodge v. Irvis* [1972]). Because of the state action requirement, the Fourteenth Amendment does not protect against discrimination in private establishments such as restaurants and hotels. Congress has been able to legislate against this kind of discrimination, however, through its authority to regulate interstate commerce and its passage of the Civil Rights Act of 1964.

The Supreme Court has developed a three-tier test of whether actions violate the equal protection clause. At the bottom, the basic test is ordinary scrutiny, whether the classification is not arbitrary, is reasonable, and has a fair and substantial relation to the object of the legislation. Ordinary scrutiny places the burden of proof on the individual challenging the law. Suspect classifications (race, religion, and ethnicity) receive strict scrutiny, which places a heavy (often fatal) burden on the government to prove that there is a compelling need for the classification and that it has drawn its legislation to be the least restrictive alternative. In *Brown v. Board of Education* (1954) the Supreme Court held that the practice of racial segregation was "inherently unequal." *Brown* withdrew all constitutional authority to use race as a criterion of exclusion, and it signaled the Court's determination to use the strict scrutiny test in cases related to racial discrimination. The Supreme Court has also used strict scrutiny in situations where some argued that race was used as a "benign" classification—where the use of race was intended to promote, rather than deny, equality. In *Parents Involved in Community Schools v. Seattle School District No. 1* (2007), the Supreme Court held that a school assignment plan that used race as a factor in order to diversify the student body of individual schools was unconstitutional. In considering affirmative action programs in university admissions, the Supreme Court has held that the use of quotas—reserving a certain number of admission places for members of a particular racial group—are unconstitutional (*Gratz v. Bollinger* [2003]) but that admissions plans that consider race as a plus factor alongside other attributes that may contribute to diversity in an educational body are narrowly tailored to the compelling interest of diversity in higher education (*Grutter v. Bollinger* [2003]). Gender classifications are tested by intermediate or heightened scrutiny, under which classifications must serve an important governmental purpose (or be supported by an "exceedingly persuasive justification") and be narrowly tailored to that purpose (*United States v. Virginia* [1996]).

Section 2

[APPORTIONMENT OF REPRESENTATIVES IN CONGRESS]
Representatives shall be apportioned among the several States according to their respective numbers, counting the whole number of persons in each State, excluding Indians not taxed. But when the right to vote at any election for the choice of electors for President and Vice-President of the United States, Representatives in Congress, the Executive and Judicial officers of a State, or the members of the Legislature thereof, is denied to any of the male inhabitants of such State, being twenty-one years of age, and citizens of the United States, or in any way abridged, except for participation in rebellion, or other crime, the basis of representation therein shall be reduced in the proportion which the number of such male citizens shall bear to the whole number of male citizens twenty-one years of age in such State.

The three-fifths clause of Article I is repealed.

Section 3

[PERSONS DISQUALIFIED FROM HOLDING OFFICE]
No person shall be a Senator or Representative in Congress, or elector of President and Vice-President, or hold any office, civil or military, under the United States, or under any State, who, having previously taken an oath, as a member of Congress, or as an officer of the United States, or as a member of any State legislature, or as an executive or judicial officer of any State, to support the Constitution of the United States, shall have engaged in insurrection or rebellion against the same, or given aid or comfort to the enemies thereof. But Congress may by a vote of two-thirds of each House, remove such disability.

Former officials of the Confederate government are prohibited from holding political office. This provision disqualified the bulk of the prewar political class and opened the way for new regimes in the defeated southern states. Within a few years, former Confederates had been pardoned, and, by the 1870s, elements of the prewar elite had regained power in most of the southern states.

Section 4

[WHAT PUBLIC DEBTS ARE VALID]
  The validity of the public debt of the United States, authorized by law, including debts incurred for payment of pensions and bounties for services in suppressing insurrection or rebellion, shall not be questioned. But neither the United States nor any State shall assume or pay any debt or obligation incurred in aid of insurrection or rebellion against the United States, or any claim for the loss or emancipation of any slave; but all such debts, obligations and claims shall be held illegal and void.

The United States would not pay debts owed by the former Confederacy, nor would former slaveholders be compensated for the loss of their slaves.

Section 5

[POWER TO ENFORCE THIS ARTICLE]
  The Congress shall have power to enforce, by appropriate legislation, the provisions of this article.

The enforcement clause gives Congress the power to override the authority of the states if needed to ensure their compliance with the Fourteenth Amendment.

AMENDMENT XV

[Proposed by Congress on February 26, 1869; declared ratified on March 30, 1870.]

Section 1

[NEGRO SUFFRAGE]
  The right of citizens of the United States to vote shall not be denied or abridged by the United States or by any State on account of race, color, or previous condition of servitude.

Section 2

[POWER TO ENFORCE THIS ARTICLE]
  The Congress shall have power to enforce this article by appropriate legislation.

The Fifteenth Amendment was designed mainly to provide voting rights to black men in the southern states who had been freed from slavery by the Thirteenth Amendment. The amendment did not address restrictions on voting rights that were not based on explicit racial criteria. Within a few years after its ratification, the Fifteenth Amendment had become a dead letter as the states of the former Confederacy adopted, as part of "Jim Crow," a host of suffrage restrictions that effectively

AMENDMENT	PURPOSE	YEAR PROPOSED	YEAR ADOPTED
Amending the Constitution to Expand the Electorate			
XV	Extended voting rights to all races	1869	1870
XIX	Extended voting rights to women	1919	1920
XXIII	Extended voting rights to residents of the District of Columbia	1960	1961
XXIV	Extended voting rights to all classes by abolition of poll taxes	1962	1964
XXVI	Extended voting rights to citizens age eighteen and over	1971	1971*

*The Twenty-Sixth Amendment holds the record for speed of adoption. It was proposed on March 23, 1971, and adopted on July 5, 1971.

disfranchised blacks without explicitly mentioning race. Not for another hundred years, until the enactment of the 1965 Voting Rights Act, did black citizens truly gain the right to vote. Initially, southern states challenged the enforcement of particular provisions of the Voting Rights Act as a violation of state sovereignty. The Supreme Court, however, decided in *South Carolina v. Katzenbach* (1966) that Section 2 of the Fifteenth Amendment gave Congress power to remedy racial discrimination in voting and that the Voting Rights Act was a "legitimate response" to the problem.

AMENDMENT XVI

[*Proposed by Congress on July 2, 1909; declared ratified on February 25, 1913.*]
[AUTHORIZING INCOME TAXES]
    The Congress shall have power to lay and collect taxes on incomes, from whatever source derived, without apportionment among the several States, and without regard to any census or enumeration.

In 1895, the Supreme Court held in *Pollock v. Farmers' Loan* that the federal income tax violated Article I, Section 9, because it was not apportioned among the states on the basis of their populations. The Sixteenth Amendment authorizes Congress to levy a tax on incomes without apportioning it among the states. Since the Sixteenth Amendment's ratification, the Supreme Court has had many more occasions to interpret the provisions of the tax code and rules of the Internal Revenue Service.

AMENDMENT XVII

[Proposed by Congress on May 13, 1912; declared ratified on May 31, 1913.]
[POPULAR ELECTION OF SENATORS]
   The Senate of the United States shall be composed of two Senators from each State, elected by the people thereof, for six years; and each Senator shall have one vote. The electors in each State shall have the qualifications requisite for electors of the most numerous branch of the State legislatures.
   When vacancies happen in the representation of any State in the Senate, the executive authority of such State shall issue writs of election to fill such vacancies: *Provided*, That the legislature of any State may empower the executive thereof to make temporary appointments until the people fill the vacancies by election as the legislature may direct.
   This amendment shall not be so construed as to affect the election or term of any Senator chosen before it becomes valid as part of the Constitution.

Article II, Section 3, provided for selection of senators by the state legislators. This language is repealed by the Seventeenth Amendment, which, in effect, allowed direct popular election of senators. This change reduced the power of the state legislatures and made the Senate a more popular body than it had been.

AMENDMENT XVIII

[Proposed by Congress December 18, 1917; declared ratified on January 29, 1919.]

Section 1

[NATIONAL LIQUOR PROHIBITION]
   After one year from the ratification of this article the manufacture, sale, or transportation of intoxicating liquors within, the importation thereof into, or the exportation thereof from the United States and all territory subject to the jurisdiction thereof for beverage purposes is hereby prohibited.

Section 2

[POWER TO ENFORCE THIS ARTICLE]
   The Congress and the several States shall have concurrent power to enforce this article by appropriate legislation.

Section 3

[RATIFICATION WITHIN SEVEN YEARS]
   This article shall be inoperative unless it shall have been ratified as an amendment to the Constitution by the legislatures of the several States, as provided in the Constitution, within seven years from the date of the submission hereof to the States by the Congress.[1]

The Eighteenth Amendment, prohibiting the manufacture and sale of alcohol, was the result of decades of temperance agitation by religious, moral, and women's groups. These groups believed that alcohol contributed to domestic violence and had experienced some success in passing Prohibition measures at the state level. The Eighteenth Amendment was the first amendment to be sent to the states for ratification with an expiration date on it. If the states had been unable to ratify the proposed amendment within seven years, it would have been dead—which is what many believe Congress wanted. Following the ratification of the amendment, Congress enacted the Volstead Act, which directed federal law enforcement agencies to enforce Prohibition. The Supreme Court rejected challenges to the constitutionality of the amendment in the *National Prohibition Cases* (1920).

AMENDMENT XIX

[Proposed by Congress on June 4, 1919; declared ratified on August 26, 1920.]
[WOMAN SUFFRAGE]
   The right of citizens of the United States to vote shall not be denied or abridged by the United States or by any State on account of sex.
   Congress shall have power to enforce this article by appropriate legislation.

The Nineteenth Amendment provides for women's suffrage. A number of women's rights organizations had campaigned for voting rights since the mid-nineteenth century, activities that were connected to the participation of women in the abolitionist movement. Prior to congressional passage of the proposed amendment, women's groups had also tried litigation as a means of securing the vote, but were unsuccessful (*Minor v. Happersett* [1875]). The Nineteenth Amendment is also called the Anthony Amendment, in recognition of women's suffrage leader Susan B. Anthony.

---

[1]Repealed by Twenty-First Amendment.

AMENDMENT XX

[Proposed by Congress on March 2, 1932; declared ratified on February 6, 1933.]

Section 1

[TERMS OF OFFICE]
The terms of the President and Vice President shall end at noon on the 20th day of January, and the terms of Senators and Representatives at noon on the 3d day of January, of the years in which such terms would have ended if this article had not been ratified; and the terms of their successors shall then begin.

Section 2

[TIME OF CONVENING CONGRESS]
The Congress shall assemble at least once in every year, and such meeting shall begin at noon on the 3d day of January, unless they shall by law appoint a different day.

Section 3

[DEATH OF PRESIDENT-ELECT]
If, at the time fixed for the beginning of the term of the President, the President elect shall have died, the Vice President elect shall become President. If a President shall not have been chosen before the time fixed for the beginning of his term, or if the President elect shall have failed to qualify, then the Vice President elect shall act as President until a President shall have qualified; and the Congress may by law provide for the case wherein neither a President elect nor a Vice President elect shall have qualified, declaring who shall then act as President, or the manner in which one who is to act shall be selected, and such person shall act accordingly until a President or Vice President shall have qualified.

Section 4

[ELECTION OF THE PRESIDENT]
The Congress may by law provide for the case of the death of any of the persons from whom the House of Representatives may choose a President whenever the right of choice shall have devolved upon them, and for the case of the death of any of the persons from whom the Senate may choose a Vice President whenever the right of choice shall have devolved upon them.

Section 5

[AMENDMENT TAKES EFFECT]
    Sections 1 and 2 shall take effect on the 15th day of October following the ratification of this article.

Section 6

[RATIFICATION WITHIN SEVEN YEARS]
    This article shall be inoperative unless it shall have been ratified as an amendment to the Constitution by the legislatures of three-fourths of the several States within seven years from the date of its submission.

The main purpose of the Twentieth Amendment was to reduce the length of time that a lame-duck president continued in office after a new president was elected. As provided by the amendment, a new president begins office on January 20 following the November election. The new Congress convenes earlier in January in case it is charged with the task of selecting the president. The amendment also establishes procedures for the selection of a president if the president-elect dies before taking office.

AMENDMENT XXI

[Proposed by Congress on February 20, 1933; declared ratified on December 5, 1933.]

Section 1

[NATIONAL LIQUOR PROHIBITION REPEALED]
    The eighteenth article of amendment to the Constitution of the United States is hereby repealed.

Section 2

[TRANSPORTATION OF LIQUOR INTO "DRY" STATES]
    The transportation or importation into any State, Territory, or Possession of the United States for delivery or use therein of intoxicating liquors, in violation of the laws thereof, is hereby prohibited.

Section 3

[RATIFICATION WITHIN SEVEN YEARS]
This article shall be inoperative unless it shall have been ratified as an amendment to the Constitution by conventions in the several States, as provided in the Constitution, within seven years from the date of the submission hereof to the States by the Congress.

Prohibition had come to be seen as a terrible failure, producing gangs of bootleggers and thugs whose murderous activities alarmed the nation. In the depths of the Great Depression, moreover, it seemed foolish to curtail the activities of one of the nation's largest industries. The Twenty-First Amendment represents the only occasion that a constitutional amendment has been repealed. Interestingly, it is also the only amendment to be ratified by voters as opposed to state legislatures; the amendment specifies that its ratification will take place through state conventions.

AMENDMENT XXII

[*Proposed by Congress on March 21, 1947; declared ratified on February 27, 1951.*]

Section 1

[TENURE OF PRESIDENT LIMITED]
No person shall be elected to the office of President more than twice, and no person who has held the office of President or acted as President, for more than two years of a term to which some other person was elected President shall be elected to the office of the President more than once. But this Article shall not apply to any person holding the office of President when this Article was proposed by the Congress, and shall not prevent any person who may be holding the office of President, or acting as President, during the term within which this Article becomes operative from holding the office of President or acting as President during the remainder of such term.

Section 2

[RATIFICATION WITHIN SEVEN YEARS]
This article shall be inoperative unless it shall have been ratified as an amendment to the Constitution by the legislatures of three-fourths of the several States within seven years from the date of its submission to the States by the Congress.

Franklin D. Roosevelt was the only U.S. president to serve more than two terms. He was elected four times, though he died in 1945 after serving only a year of his last term. When Republicans took control of Congress in 1946, they were determined to prevent a future Democrat from occupying the White House for multiple terms and so pushed through the Twenty-Second Amendment. Years later, when a popular Republican, Ronald Reagan, occupied the White House, the GOP had second thoughts about the wisdom of the Twenty-Second Amendment. The Supreme Court has held that provisions in state constitutions that limit the number of terms a person can be elected to the U.S. Congress violate the U.S. Constitution because they modify the requirements set out for election to Congress in Article I (*U.S. Term Limits v. Thornton* [1995]). A new constitutional amendment would be needed in order to limit the numbers of terms a representative or senator could serve.

AMENDMENT XXIII

[Proposed by Congress on June 16, 1960; declared ratified on March 29, 1961.]

Section 1

[ELECTORAL COLLEGE VOTES FOR THE DISTRICT OF COLUMBIA]
    The District constituting the seat of Government of the United States shall appoint in such manner as the Congress may direct:
    A number of electors of President and Vice President equal to the whole number of Senators and Representatives in Congress to which the District would be entitled if it were a State, but in no event more than the least populous State; they shall be in addition to those appointed by the States, but they shall be considered, for the purposes of the election of President and Vice President, to be electors appointed by a State; and they shall meet in the District and perform such duties as provided by the twelfth article of amendment.

Section 2

[POWER TO ENFORCE THIS ARTICLE]
    The Congress shall have power to enforce this article by appropriate legislation.

Residents of the District of Columbia do not elect senators or representatives, but the Twenty-Third Amendment allows them to participate in presidential elections by choosing presidential electors. Many individuals advocate full voting rights for District residents, but since the District is solidly Democratic, voting rights would mean two more Democratic senators and several Democratic House members. Republicans are reluctant to allow this change in the balance of congressional power. Additionally, the District's neighbors generally oppose such a move, regardless of party lines; statehood for DC might allow it to pass a "commuter tax" on those who work in DC but live in Maryland and Virginia suburbs.

AMENDMENT XXIV

[Proposed by Congress on August 27, 1962; declared ratified on January 23, 1964.]

Section 1

[ANTI-POLL TAX]
The right of citizens of the United States to vote in any primary or other election for President or Vice President, for electors for President or Vice President, or for Senator or Representative of Congress, shall not be denied or abridged by the United States or any State by reason of failure to pay any poll tax or other tax.

Section 2

[POWER TO ENFORCE THIS ARTICLE]
The Congress shall have power to enforce this article by appropriate legislation.

Poll taxes were one of the tools used by southern voting registrars to circumvent the Fifteenth Amendment. For the most part, the tax was enforced only against blacks, and its elimination was a major step in the direction of voting rights for blacks in the 1960s. The amendment does not explicitly prohibit use of poll taxes in state elections. In *Harper v. Virginia Board of Elections* (1966), the Supreme Court interpreted it and the equal protection clause to extend to ending that practice as well.

AMENDMENT XXV

[Proposed by Congress on July 6, 1965; declared ratified on February 10, 1967.]

Section 1

[VICE PRESIDENT TO BECOME PRESIDENT]
In case of the removal of the President from office or his death or resignation, the Vice President shall become President.

Section 2

[CHOICE OF A NEW VICE PRESIDENT]
Whenever there is a vacancy in the office of the Vice President, the President shall nominate a Vice President who shall take the office upon confirmation by a majority vote of both houses of Congress.

Section 3

[PRESIDENT MAY DECLARE OWN DISABILITY]
Whenever the President transmits to the President pro tempore of the Senate and the Speaker of the House of Representatives his written declaration that he is unable to discharge the powers and duties of his office, and until he transmits to them a written declaration to the contrary, such powers and duties shall be discharged by the Vice President as Acting President.

Section 4

[ALTERNATE PROCEDURES TO DECLARE AND TO END PRESIDENTIAL DISABILITY]
Whenever the Vice President and a majority of either the principal officers of the executive departments, or of such other body as Congress may by law provide, transmit to the President pro tempore of the Senate and the Speaker of the House of Representatives their written declaration that the President is unable to discharge the powers and duties of his office, the Vice President shall immediately assume the powers and duties of the office as Acting President.

Thereafter, when the President transmits to the President pro tempore of the Senate and the Speaker of the House of Representatives his written declaration that no inability exists, he shall resume the powers and duties of his office unless the Vice President and a majority of either the principal officers of the executive department, or of such other body as Congress may by law provide, transmit within four days to the President pro tempore of the Senate and the Speaker of the House of Representatives their written declaration that the President is unable to discharge the powers and duties of his office. Thereupon Congress shall decide the issue, assembling within forty eight hours for that purpose if not in session. If the Congress, within twenty one days after receipt of the latter written declaration, or, if Congress is not in session, within twenty one days after Congress is required to assemble, determines by two-thirds vote of both Houses that the President is unable to discharge the powers and duties of his office, the Vice President shall continue to discharge the same as Acting President; otherwise, the President shall resume the powers and duties of his office.

The Twenty-Fifth Amendment affirms that the vice president succeeds to the presidency if the president dies, leaves office, or is disabled. The amendment also stipulates that the president is to select a vice president—with congressional approval—if the office of the vice presidency becomes vacant. If the president is temporarily disabled, he may transfer authority to the vice president. President Reagan temporarily transferred authority to Vice President George H. W. Bush when Reagan underwent surgery. President George W. Bush also transferred power to Vice President Dick Cheney when Bush underwent minor surgery. The president may also be removed if he is deemed by the vice president and a majority of cabinet members to be disabled. The Constitution provides for the vice president to succeed the president, if needed. The Presidential Succession Act of 1947 determines the order in which other federal officials would assume the office if the vice presidency were vacant. Following the vice president are the Speaker of the House, the President Pro Tempore of the Senate, and members of the Cabinet (ranked in order of the number of years their department has existed). To assume the presidency, each official must meet the Constitution's qualifications of age and citizenship to serve as president. For example, during the presidency of Bill Clinton, Secretary of State Madeleine Albright would have been ineligible to succeed the president because she is not a natural-born citizen of the United States.

AMENDMENT XXVI

[Proposed by Congress on March 23, 1971; declared ratified on July 1, 1971.]

Section 1

[EIGHTEEN-YEAR-OLD VOTE]
The right of citizens of the United States, who are eighteen years of age or older, to vote shall not be denied or abridged by the United States or by any State on account of age.

Section 2

[POWER TO ENFORCE THIS ARTICLE]
The Congress shall have power to enforce this article by appropriate legislation.

The minimum age of voters in federal elections was reduced to eighteen. Previously, Congress had tried to lower the voting age by statute, but the Supreme Court held that Congress had the authority to do so only for federal elections. This presented a situation in which eighteen year olds might be able to vote for president, but not for their mayor or governor, depending on the laws of their home state. Opponents of the Vietnam War hoped that draft-age men would be able to voice their opposition to the war. Democrats, believing that most young people would support them, were especially supportive of this amendment. For much of the 1980s, voter turnout among eighteen-to twenty-five-year olds remained low, leading candidates to adopt strategies to mobilize this age bracket and to the birth of voter registration drives like MTV's "Rock the Vote." These drives have helped increase the youth vote in every election since 2004. The Obama campaign made young voters central to its 2008 electoral strategy. The youth vote increased slightly in 2008 when 66 percent of younger voters cast their ballots for Barack Obama.

AMENDMENT XXVII

[Proposed by Congress on September 25, 1789; declared ratified on May 8, 1992.]
[CONGRESS CANNOT RAISE ITS OWN PAY]
   No law varying the compensation for the services of the Senators and Representatives, shall take effect, until an election of representatives shall have intervened.

During the 1990s, many Americans believed that members of Congress often engaged in self-serving conduct. The idea of prohibiting members of Congress from raising their own salaries had actually been proposed as one of the original amendments to the Constitution but was not ratified by three-fourths of the states and had been forgotten for nearly two hundred years until University of Texas students read about the proposal and launched a campaign to bring it back to life.

WHAT'S NOT IN THE CONSTITUTION?

Several familiar components of our modern-day political system do not appear at all in the Constitution. As our discussion of the Ninth Amendment mentioned, one of those is the right to privacy. What other facets of the American democratic system are not listed in the constitutional text?
   * *Political Parties:* Constitutionally, parties are essentially voluntary associations. For this reason, the Supreme Court has voided state laws that interfere with party activities and rules. Yet parties have played an integral role in American political development historically and contemporarily, something that is recognized by the Court. Thus, the Court has been unfriendly to allowing party practices that interfere with the individual exercise of voting rights and political participation, such as laws that designated all-white primaries or restrictions on campaign donations.
   * *The Cabinet:* Article II, Section 2, implies that the president may utilize offices and advisors to assist in the enforcement of the nation's laws, but does not specify which or how many executive departments may be created. Unlike comparable structures in other countries, the American Cabinet is not a collective group, but is instead an advisory body for the president. Appointments must be approved by the Senate, but are not responsible to the Senate or to Congress at large.
   * *Judicial Review:* The power of the courts to declare invalid the actions of the legislative and executive branches or of the states is not explicitly mentioned in the Constitution. This major power of the federal judiciary is accepted today as natural and practical, but is subject to the limitations judges place on themselves and by judicial dependence on the other branches to enforce and abide by their decisions.
   * *The Jury:* Of course the Constitution makes provisions for juries, but not in the way most people imagine. Commonly, the right to a jury trial is often expressed as "the right to a jury of one's peers." Actually, the Constitution says little about the specific make-up of juries. The Constitution says only that the accused shall enjoy

a right to trial "by an impartial jury of the State and district" in which the crime was committed. Juries are expected to be drawn from a cross-section of the community, based on principles enunciated in Supreme Court decisions *Batson v. Kentucky* (1986) and *J.E.B. v. Alabama ex rel. T.B.* (1994).

* *Travel:* Another protection widely assumed but not mentioned in the Constitution is the right to travel. Such a right may be implied by Article IV, Section 2's discussion of comity and its limitation of travel by criminal suspects and fugitives. In *Kent v. Dulles* (1958) the Supreme Court determined the right to travel was a natural right and thus invalidated State Department restrictions on issuing passports to citizens with particular political affiliations, such as with the Communist Party.

* *Key Quotes:* Many well-known phrases of American politics and history are associated with but appear nowhere in the Constitution. Many of these phrases appear in other major American historical documents. Among such phrases are "a wall of separation" between church and state (popularized by Thomas Jefferson's writings), "of the people, by the people, for the people" (Gettysburg Address), and "life, liberty, and the pursuit of happiness" (Declaration of Independence).

The Declaration of Independence

The Declaration of Independence is a statement of American colonial independence from British rule. Written by Thomas Jefferson and adopted by the Second Continental Congress, the Declaration of Independence was an extraordinary document in both philosophical and political terms. In philosophic terms, the Declaration was remarkable for its assertion that certain rights, called "unalienable rights"—including life, liberty, and the pursuit of happiness—could not be abridged by governments. In the world of 1776, a world in which some kings still claimed to rule by divine right, this was a dramatic statement. In political terms, the Declaration was remarkable because, despite the differences of interest that divided the colonists along economic, regional, and philosophical lines, it identified and focused on problems, grievances, aspirations, and principles that might unify the various colonial groups. In its time, the Declaration was an attempt to identify and articulate a history and set of principles that might help to forge national unity.

Since the Founding, the ideals expressed in the Declaration have served as an inspiration for groups seeking inclusion and equality in American politics and society. In 1848, the first Women's Rights Convention wrote a Declaration of Sentiments based on the Declaration of Independence that argued that "all men and women are created equal," and that, among other rights, women were entitled to vote. Martin Luther King, Jr., in the famous "I have a dream" speech, referred to the Declaration of Independence as a "promissory note" and dreamed that the United States would "rise up and live out the true meaning of its creed: 'We hold these truths to be self-evident: that all men are created equal.' "

In Congress, July 4, 1776
The unanimous Declaration of the thirteen united States of America,

63

When in the Course of human events, it becomes necessary for one people to dissolve the political bands which have connected them with another, and to assume among the powers of the earth, the separate and equal station to which the Laws of Nature and of Nature's God entitle them, a decent respect to the opinions of mankind requires that they should declare the causes which impel them to the separation.

We hold these truths to be self-evident, that all men are created equal, that they are endowed by their Creator with certain unalienable Rights, that among these are Life, Liberty and the pursuit of Happiness.—That to secure these rights, Governments are instituted among Men, deriving their just powers from the consent of the governed.—That whenever any Form of Government becomes destructive of these ends, it is the Right of the People to alter or to abolish it, and to institute new Government, laying its foundation on such principles and organizing its powers in such form, as to them shall seem most likely to effect their Safety and Happiness. Prudence, indeed, will dictate that Governments long established should not be changed for light and transient causes; and accordingly all experience hath shewn, that mankind are more disposed to suffer, while evils are sufferable, than to right themselves by abolishing the forms to which they are accustomed. But when a long train of abuses and usurpations, pursuing invariably the same Object evinces a design to reduce them under absolute Despotism, it is their right, it is their duty, to throw off such Government, and to provide new Guards for their future security.—Such has been the patient sufferance of these Colonies; and such is now the necessity which constrains them to alter their former Systems of Government. The history of the present King of Great Britain is a history of repeated injuries and usurpations, all having in direct object the establishment of an absolute Tyranny over these States. To prove this, let Facts be submitted to a candid world.

He has refused his Assent to Laws, the most wholesome and necessary for the public good.

He has forbidden his Governors to pass Laws of immediate and pressing importance, unless suspended in their operation till his Assent should be obtained; and when so suspended, he has utterly neglected to attend to them.

He has refused to pass other Laws for the accommodation of large districts of people, unless those people would relinquish the right of Representation in the Legislature, a right inestimable to them and formidable to tyrants only.

He has called together legislative bodies at places unusual, uncomfortable, and distant from the depository of their public Records, for the sole purpose of fatiguing them into compliance with his measures.

He has dissolved Representative Houses repeatedly, for opposing with manly firmness his invasions on the rights of the people.

He has refused for a long time, after such dissolutions, to cause others to be elected; whereby the Legislative powers, incapable of Annihilation, have returned to the People at large for their exercise; the State remaining in the mean time exposed to all the dangers of invasion from without, and convulsions within.

He has endeavoured to prevent the population of these States; for that purpose obstructing the Laws for Naturalization of Foreigners; refusing to pass others to encourage their migrations hither, and raising the conditions of new Appropriations of Lands.

He has obstructed the Administration of Justice, by refusing his Assent to Laws for establishing Judiciary powers.

He has made Judges dependent on his Will alone, for the tenure of their offices, and the amount and payment of their salaries.

He has erected a multitude of New Offices, and sent hither swarms of Officers to harrass our people, and eat out their substance.

He has kept among us, in times of peace, Standing Armies without the Consent of our legislatures.

He has affected to render the Military independent of and superior to the Civil power.

He has combined with others to subject us to a jurisdiction foreign to our constitution, and unacknowledged by our laws; giving his Assent to their Acts of pretended Legislation:

For Quartering large bodies of armed troops among us:

For protecting them, by a mock Trial, from punishment for any Murders which they should commit on the Inhabitants of these States:

For cutting off our Trade with all parts of the world:

For imposing Taxes on us without our Consent:

For depriving us in many cases, of the benefits of Trial by Jury:

For transporting us beyond Seas to be tried for pretended offences:

For abolishing the free System of English Laws in a neighboring Province, establishing therein an Arbitrary government, and enlarging its Boundaries so as to render it at once an example and fit instrument for introducing the same absolute rule into these Colonies:

For taking away our Charters, abolishing our most valuable Laws, and altering fundamentally the Forms of our Governments:

For suspending our own Legislatures, and declaring themselves invested with power to legislate for us in all cases whatsoever.

He has abdicated Government here, by declaring us out of his Protection and waging War against us.

He has plundered our seas, ravaged our Coasts, burnt our towns, and destroyed the lives of our people.

He is at this time transporting large Armies of foreign Mercenaries to compleat the works of death, desolation and tyranny, already begun with circumstances of Cruelty & perfidy scarcely paralleled in the most barbarous ages, and totally unworthy the Head of a civilized nation.

He has constrained our fellow Citizens taken Captive on the high Seas to bear Arms against their Country, to become the executioners of their friends and Brethren, or to fall themselves by their Hands.

He has excited domestic insurrections amongst us, and has endeavoured to bring on the inhabitants of our frontiers, the merciless Indian Savages, whose known rule of warfare, is an undistinguished destruction of all ages, sexes and conditions.

In every stage of these Oppressions We have Petitioned for Redress in the most humble terms: Our repeated Petitions have been answered only by repeated injury. A Prince whose character is thus marked by every act which may define a Tyrant, is unfit to be the ruler of a free people.

Nor have We been wanting in attentions to our Brittish brethren. We have warned them from time to time of attempts by their legislature to extend an unwarrantable jurisdiction over us. We have reminded them of the circumstances of our emigration and settlement here. We have appealed to their native justice and magnanimity, and we have conjured them by the ties of our common kindred to disavow these usurpations, which, would inevitably interrupt our connections and correspondence. They too have been deaf to the voice of justice and of consanguinity. We must, therefore, acquiesce in the necessity, which denounces our Separation, and hold them, as we hold the rest of mankind, Enemies in War, in Peace Friends.

We, Therefore, the Representatives of the United States of America, in General Congress, Assembled, appealing to the Supreme Judge of the world for the rectitude of our intentions, do, in the Name, and by Authority of the good People of these Colonies, solemnly publish and declare, That these United Colonies are, and of Right ought to be Free and Independent States; that they are Absolved from all Allegiance to the British Crown, and that all political connection between them and the State of Great Britain, is and ought to be totally dissolved; and that as Free and Independent States, they have full Power to levy War, conclude Peace, contract Alliances, establish Commerce, and to do all other Acts and Things which Independent States may of right do. And for the support of this Declaration, with a firm reliance on the protection of divine Providence, we mutually pledge to each other our Lives, our Fortunes and our sacred Honor.

The foregoing Declaration was, by order of Congress, engrossed, and signed by the following members:

John Hancock

NEW HAMPSHIRE
Josiah Bartlett
William Whipple
Matthew Thornton

MASSACHUSETTS BAY
Samuel Adams
John Adams
Robert Treat Paine
Elbridge Gerry

RHODE ISLAND
Stephen Hopkins
William Ellery

CONNECTICUT
Roger Sherman
Samuel Huntington
William Williams
Oliver Wolcott

NEW YORK
William Floyd
Philip Livingston
Francis Lewis
Lewis Morris

NEW JERSEY
Richard Stockton
John Witherspoon
Francis Hopkinson
John Hart
Abraham Clark

PENNSYLVANIA
Robert Morris
Benjamin Rush
Benjamin Franklin
John Morton
George Clymer
James Smith
George Taylor
James Wilson
George Ross

DELAWARE
Caesar Rodney
George Read
Thomas M'Kean

MARYLAND
Samuel Chase
William Paca
Thomas Stone
Charles Carroll,
   of Carrollton

VIRGINIA
George Wythe
Richard Henry Lee
Thomas Jefferson
Benjamin Harrison
Thomas Nelson, Jr.
Francis Lightfoot Lee
Carter Braxton

NORTH CAROLINA
William Hooper
Joseph Hewes
John Penn

SOUTH CAROLINA
Edward Rutledge
Thomas Heyward, Jr.
Thomas Lynch, Jr.
Arthur Middleton

GEORGIA
Button Gwinnett
Lyman Hall
George Walton

Resolved, That copies of the Declaration be sent to the several assemblies, conventions, and committees, or councils of safety, and to the several commanding officers of the continental troops; that it be proclaimed in each of the United States, at the head of the army.

The Articles of Confederation

The Articles of Confederation served as the United States' first written constitution and governed the country until March 1789. Almost from their beginning, the Articles were considered in need of reform and strengthening because the central government created under the Article was very weak. The Articles were concerned with limiting the authority of the central government and preserving state sovereignty. Congress had few powers and was dependent on the states to execute its laws. Each state had one vote in Congress and the agreement of every state was necessary to amend the Articles. Because Congress could not enforce treaties, foreign countries often negotiated with individual states directly and took advantage of competition between the states. This international weakness as well as domestic economic turmoil led to calls to amend, and ultimately discard, the Articles of Confederation.

Agreed to by Congress November 15, 1777; ratified and in force March 1, 1781
  To all whom these Presents shall come, we the undersigned Delegates of the States affixed to our Names, send greeting. Whereas the Delegates of the United States of America, in Congress assembled, did, on the fifteenth day of November, in the Year of Our Lord One thousand Seven Hundred and Seventy seven, and in the Second Year of the Independence of America, agree to certain articles of Confederation and perpetual Union between the States of Newhampshire, Massachusetts-bay, Rhodeisland and Providence Plantations, Connecticut, New-York, New-Jersey, Pennsylvania, Delaware, Maryland, Virginia, North-Carolina, South-Carolina and Georgia in the words following, viz. "Articles of Confederation and perpetual Union between the states of Newhampshire, Massachusettsbay, Rhodeisland and Providence Plantations, Connecticut, New-York, New-Jersey, Pennsylvania, Delaware, Maryland, Virginia, North-Carolina, South-Carolina and Georgia.

Art. I. The Stile of this confederacy shall be "The United States of America."

Art. II. Each state retains its sovereignty, freedom and independence, and every Power, Jurisdiction and right, which is not by this confederation expressly delegated to the United States, in Congress assembled.

Art. III. The said states hereby severally enter into a firm league of friendship with each other, for their common defence, the security of their Liberties, and their mutual and general welfare, binding themselves to assist each other, against all force offered to, or attacks made upon them, or any of them, on account of religion, sovereignty, trade, or any other pretence whatever.

Art. IV. The better to secure and perpetuate mutual friendship and intercourse among the people of the different states in this union, the free inhabitants of each of these states, paupers, vagabonds and fugitives from Justice excepted, shall be entitled to all privileges and immunities of free citizens in the several states; and the people of each state shall have free ingress and regress to and from any other state, and shall enjoy therein all the privileges of trade and commerce, subject to the same duties, impositions and restrictions as the inhabitants thereof respectively, provided that such restriction shall not extend so far as to prevent the removal of property imported into any state, to any other state, of which the Owner is an inhabitant; provided also that no imposition, duties or restriction shall be laid by any state, on the property of the united states, or either of them.

If any Person guilty of, or charged with treason, felony, or other high misdemeanor in any state, shall flee from Justice, and be found in any of the united states, he shall, upon demand of the Governor or executive power, of the state from which he fled, be delivered up and removed to the state having jurisdiction of his offence.

Full faith and credit shall be given in each of these states to the records, acts and judicial proceedings of the courts and magistrates of every other state.

Art. V. For the more convenient management of the general interests of the united states, delegates shall be annually appointed in such manner as the legislature of each state shall direct, to meet in Congress on the first Monday in November, in every year, with a power reserved to each state, to recall its delegates, or any of them, at any time within the year, and to send others in their stead, for the remainder of the Year.

No state shall be represented in Congress by less than two, nor by more than seven Members; and no person shall be capable of being a delegate for more than three years in any term of six years; nor shall any person, being a delegate, be capable of holding any office under the united states, for which he, or another for his benefit receives any salary, fees or emolument of any kind.

Each state shall maintain its own delegates in a meeting of the states, and while they act as members of the committee of the states.

In determining questions in the united states, in Congress assembled, each state shall have one vote.

Freedom of speech and debate in Congress shall not be impeached or questioned in any Court, or place out of Congress, and the members of congress shall be protected in their persons from arrests and imprisonments, during the time of their going to and from, and attendance on congress, except for treason, felony, or breach of the peace.

Art. VI. No state without the Consent of the united states in congress assembled, shall send any embassy to, or receive any embassy from, or enter into any conference, agreement, or alliance or treaty with any King, prince or state; nor shall any person holding any office or profit or trust under the united states, or any of them, accept of any present, emolument, office or title of any kind whatever from any king, prince or foreign state; nor shall the united states in congress assembled, or any of them, grant any title of nobility.

No two or more states shall enter into any treaty, confederation or alliance whatever between them, without the consent of the united states in congress assembled, specifying accurately the purposes for which the same is to be entered into, and how long it shall continue.

No state shall lay any imposts or duties, which may interfere with any stipulations in treaties, entered into by the united states in congress assembled, with any king, prince or state, in pursuance of any treaties already proposed by congress, to the courts of France and Spain.

No vessels of war shall be kept up in time of peace by any state, except such number only, as shall be deemed necessary by the united states in congress assembled, for the defence of such state, or its trade; nor shall any body of forces be kept up by any state, in time of peace, except such number only, as in the judgment of the united states, in congress assembled, shall be deemed requisite to garrison the forts necessary for the defence of such state; but every state shall always keep up a well regulated and disciplined militia, sufficiently armed and accoutred, and shall provide and constantly have ready for use, in public stores, a due number of field pieces and tents, and a proper quantity of arms, ammunition and camp equipage.

No state shall engage in any war without the consent of the united states in congress assembled, unless such state be actually invaded by enemies, or shall have received certain advice of a resolution being formed by some nation of Indians to invade such state, and the danger is so imminent as not to admit of a delay, till the united states in congress asssembled can be consulted; nor shall any state grant commissions to any ships or vessels of war, nor letters of marque or reprisal, except it be after a declaration of war by the united states in congress assembled, and then only against the kingdom or state and the subjects thereof, against which war has been so declared, and under such regulations as shall be established by the united states in congress assembled, unless such state be infested by pirates; in which case vessels of war may be fitted out for that occasion, and kept so long as the danger shall continue, or until the united states in congress assembled shall determine otherwise.

Art. VII. When land-forces are raised by any state for the common defence, all officers of or under the rank of colonel, shall be appointed by the legislature of each state respectively, by whom such forces shall be raised, or in such manner as such state shall direct, and all vacancies shall be filled up by the state which first made the appointment.

Art. VIII. All charges of war, and all other expences that shall be incurred for the common defence or general welfare, and allowed by the united states in congress assembled, shall be defrayed out of a common treasury, which shall be supplied by the several states in proportion to the value of all land within each state, granted to or surveyed for any Person, as such land and the buildings and improvements thereon shall be estimated according to such mode as the united states in congress assembled, shall from time to time direct and appoint.

The taxes for paying that proportion shall be laid and levied by the authority and direction of the legislatures of the several states within the time agreed upon by the united states in congress assembled.

Art. IX. The united states in congress assembled, shall have the sole and exclusive right and power of determining on peace and war, except in the cases mentioned in the sixth article—of sending and receiving ambassadors—entering into treaties and alliances, provided that no treaty of commerce shall be made whereby the legislative power of the respective states shall be restrained from imposing such imposts and duties on foreigners, as their own people are subjected to, or from prohibiting the exportation of any species of goods or commodities whatsoever—of establishing rules for deciding in all cases, what captures on land or water shall be legal, and in what manner prizes taken by land or naval forces in the service of the united states shall be divided or appropriated—of granting letters of marque and reprisal in times of peace—appointing courts for the trial of piracies and felonies committed on the high seas and establishing courts for receiving and determining finally appeals in all cases of captures, provided that no member of congress shall be appointed a judge of any of the said courts.

The united states in congress assembled shall also be the last resort on appeal in all disputes and differences now subsisting or that hereafter may arise between two or more states concerning boundary, jurisdiction or any other cause whatever; which authority shall always be exercised in the manner following. Whenever the legislative or executive authority or lawful agent of any state in controversy with another shall present a petition to congress stating the matter in question and praying for a hearing, notice thereof shall be given by order of congress to the legislative or executive authority of the other state in controversy, and a day assigned for the appearance of the parties by their lawful agents, who shall then be directed to appoint by joint consent, commissioners or judges to constitute a court for hearing and determining the matter in question: but if they cannot agree, congress shall name three persons out of each of the united states, and from the list of such persons each party shall alternately strike out one, the petitioners beginning, until the number shall be reduced to thirteen; and from that number not less than seven, nor more than nine names as congress shall direct, shall in the presence of congress be drawn out by lot, and the persons whose names shall be so drawn or any five of them, shall be commissioners or judges, to hear and finally determine the controversy, so always as a major part of the judges who shall hear the cause shall agree in the determination: and if either party shall neglect to attend at the day appointed, without shewing reasons, which congress shall judge sufficient, or being present shall refuse to strike, the congress shall proceed to nominate three persons out of each state, and the secretary of congress shall strike in behalf of such party absent or refusing; and the judgment and sentence of the court to be appointed, in the manner before prescribed, shall be final and conclusive; and if any of the parties shall refuse to submit to the authority of such court, or to appear to defend their claim or cause, the court shall nevertheless proceed to pronounce sentence, or judgment, which shall in like manner be final and decisive, the judgment or sentence and other proceedings being in either case transmitted to congress, and lodged among the acts of congress for the security of the parties concerned: provided that every commissioner, before he sits in judgment, shall take an oath to be administered by one of the judges of the supreme or superior court of the state, where the cause shall be tried, "well and truly to hear and determine the matter in question, according to the best of his judgment, without favour, affection or hope of reward:" provided also, that no state shall be deprived of territory for the benefit of the united states.

All controversies concerning the private right of soil claimed under different grants of two or more states, whose jurisdictions as they may respect such lands, and the states which passed such grants are adjusted, the said grants or either of them being at the same time claimed to have originated antecedent to such settlement of jurisdiction, shall on the petition of either party to the congress of the united states, be finally determined as near as may be in the same manner as is before prescribed for deciding disputes respecting territorial jurisdiction between different states.

The united states in congress assembled shall also have the sole and exclusive right and power of regulating the alloy and value of coin struck by their own authority, or by that of the respective states—fixing the standard of weights and measures throughout the united states—regulating the trade and managing all affairs with the Indians, not members of any of the states, provided that the legislative right of any state within its own limits be not infringed or violated—establishing and regulating post-offices from one state to another, throughout all the united states, and exacting such postage on the papers passing thro' the same as may be requisite to defray the expences of the said office—appointing all officers of the land forces, in the service of the united states, excepting regimental officers—appointing all the officers of the naval forces, and commissioning all officers whatever in the service of the united states—making rules for the government and regulation of the said land and naval forces, and directing their operations.

The united states in congress assembled shall have authority to appoint a committee, to sit in the recess of congress, to be denominated "A Committee of the States," and to consist of one delegate from each state; and to appoint such other committees and civil officers as may be necessary for managing the general affairs of the united states under their direction—to appoint one of their number to preside, provided that no person be allowed to serve in the office of president more than one year in any term of three years; to ascertain the necessary sums of Money to be raised for the service of the united states, and to appropriate and apply the same for defraying the public expenses—to borrow money, or emit bills on the credit of the united states, transmitting every half year to the respective states an account of the sums of money so borrowed or emitted,—to build and equip a navy—to agree upon the number of land forces, and to make requisitions from each state for its quota, in proportion to the number of white inhabitants in such state; which requisition shall be binding, and thereupon the legislature of each state shall appoint the regimental officers, raise the men and cloath, arm and equip then in a soldier like manner, at the expense of the united states; and the officers and men so cloathed, armed and equipped shall march to the place appointed, and within the time agreed on by the united states in congress assembled: But if the united states in congress assembled shall, on consideration of circumstances judge proper that any state should not raise men, or should raise a smaller number than its quota, and that any other state should raise a greater number of men than the quota thereof, such extra number shall be raised, officered, cloathed, armed and equipped in the same manner as the quota of such state, unless the legislature of such state shall judge that such extra number cannot be safely spared out of the same, in which case they shall raise officer, cloath, arm and equip as many of such extra number as they judge can be safely spared. And the officers and men so cloathed, armed and equipped, shall march to the place appointed, and within the time agreed on by the united states in congress assembled.

The united states in congress assembled shall never engage in a war, nor grant letters of marque and reprisal in time of peace, nor enter into any treaties or alliances, nor coin money, nor regulate the value thereof, nor ascertain the sums and expenses necessary for the defence and welfare of the united states, or any of them, nor emit bills, nor borrow money on the credit of the united states, nor appropriate money, nor agree upon the number of vessels of war, to be built or purchased, or the number of land or sea forces to be raised, nor appoint a commander in chief of the army or navy, unless nine states assent to the same: nor shall a question on any other point, except for adjourning from day to day be determined, unless by the votes of a majority of the united states in congress assembled.

The congress of the united states shall have power to adjourn to any time within the year, and to any place within the united states, so that no period of adjournment be for a longer duration than the space of six Months, and shall publish the Journal of their proceedings monthly, except such parts thereof relating to treaties, alliances or military operations, as in their judgment require secrecy; and the yeas and nays of the delegates of each state on any question shall be entered on the Journal, when it is desired by any delegate; and the delegates of a state, or any of them, at his or their request shall be furnished with a transcript of the said Journal, except such parts as are above excepted, to lay before the legislatures of the several states.

Art. X. The committee of the states, or any nine of them, shall be authorised to execute, in the recess of congress, such of the powers of congress as the united states in congress assembled, by the consent of nine states, shall from time to time think expedient to vest them with; provided that no power be delegated to the said committee, for the exercise of which, by the articles of confederation, the voice of nine states in the congress of the united states assembled is requisite.

Art. XI. Canada acceding to this confederation, and joining in the measures of the united states, shall be admitted into, and entitled to all the advantages of this union: but no other colony shall be admitted into the same, unless such admission be agreed to by nine states.

Art. XII. All bills of credit emitted, monies borrowed and debts contracted by, or under the authority of congress, before the assembling of the united states, in pursuance of the present confederation, shall be deemed and considered as a charge against the united states, for payment and satisfaction whereof the said united states and the public faith are hereby solemnly pledged.

Art. XIII. Every state shall abide by the determinations of the united states in congress assembled, on all questions which by this confederation are submitted to them. And the Articles of this confederation shall be inviolably observed by every state, and the union shall be perpetual; nor shall any alteration at any time hereafter be made in any of them; unless such alteration be agreed to in a congress of the united states, and be afterwards confirmed by the legislatures of every state.

And Whereas it hath pleased the Great Governor of the World to incline the hearts of the legislatures we respectively represent in congress, to approve of, and to authorize us to ratify the said articles of confederation and perpetual union. Know Ye that we the undersigned delegates, by virtue of the power and authority to us given for that purpose, do by these presents, in the name and in behalf of our respective constituents, fully and entirely ratify and confirm each and every of the said articles of confederation and perpetual union, and all and singular the matters and things therein contained: And we do further solemnly plight and engage the faith of our respective constituents, that they shall abide by the determinations of the united states in congress assembled, on all questions, which by the said confederation are submitted to them. And that the articles thereof shall be inviolably observed by the states we respectively represent, and that the union shall be perpetual. In Witness whereof we have hereunto set our hands in Congress. Done at Philadelphia in the state of Pennsylvania the ninth day of July, in the Year of our Lord one Thousand seven Hundred and Seventy-eight, and in the third year of the independence of America.

The Federalist Papers

During the ratification struggle, thousands of essays, speeches, pamphlets, and letters were presented in support of and in opposition to the proposed Constitution. The best-known pieces supporting ratification of the Constitution were the eighty-five essays written under the name of "Publius," by Alexander Hamilton, James Madison, and John Jay between the fall of 1787 and the spring of 1788. *The Federalist Papers*, as they are collectively known today, defended the principles of the Constitution and sought to dispel fears of a national authority. The two essays here were both written by James Madison. In "Federalist No. 10," Madison advocates political pluralism as a means of countering those groups, or factions, whose wishes would infringe on the rights of other citizens or would not be to the benefit of the whole community. In "Federalist No. 51," Madison addresses the system of checks and balances as a way of limiting power within the national government and controlling individual political ambition.

NO. 10: MADISON

Among the numerous advantages promised by a well constructed Union, none deserves to be more accurately developed than its tendency to break and control the violence of faction. The friend of popular governments never finds himself so much alarmed for their character and fate, as when he contemplates their propensity to this dangerous vice. He will not fail therefore to set a due value on any plan which, without violating the principles to which he is attached, provides a proper cure for it. The instability, injustice, and confusion introduced into the public councils have, in truth, been the mortal diseases under which popular governments have everywhere perished, as they continue to be the favorite and fruitful topics from which the adversaries to liberty derive their most specious declamations. The valuable improvements made by the American constitutions on the popular models, both ancient and modern, cannot certainly be too much admired; but it would be an unwarrantable partiality to contend that they have as effectually obviated the danger on this side, as was wished and expected. Complaints are everywhere heard from our most considerate and virtuous citizens, equally the friends of public and private faith and of public and personal liberty, that our governments are too unstable, that the public good is disregarded in the conflicts of rival parties, and that measures are too often decided, not according to the rules of justice and the rights of the minor party, but by the superior force of an interested and overbearing majority. However anxiously we may wish that these complaints had no foundation, the evidence of known facts will not permit us to deny that they are in some degree true. It will be found, indeed, on a candid review of our situation, that some of the distresses under which we labor have been erroneously charged on the operation of our governments; but it will be found, at the same time, that other causes will not alone account for many of our heaviest misfortunes; and, particularly, for that prevailing and increasing distrust of public engagements and alarm for private rights which are echoed from one end of the continent to the other. These must be chiefly, if not wholly, effects of the unsteadiness and injustice with which a factious spirit has tainted our public administration.

By a faction I understand a number of citizens, whether amounting to a majority or minority of the whole, who are united and actuated by some common impulse of passion, or of interest, adverse to the rights of other citizens, or to the permanent and aggregate interests of the community.

There are two methods of curing the mischiefs of faction: the one, by removing its causes; the other, by controlling its effects.

There are again two methods of removing the causes of faction: the one, by destroying the liberty which is essential to its existence; the other, by giving to every citizen the same opinions, the same passions, and the same interests.

It could never be more truly said than of the first remedy, that it is worse than the disease. Liberty is to faction what air is to fire, an aliment without which it instantly expires. But it could not be a less folly to abolish liberty, which is essential to political life, because it nourishes faction, than it would be to wish the annihilation of air, which is essential to animal life, because it imparts to fire its destructive agency.

The second expedient is as impracticable, as the first would be unwise. As long as the reason of man continues fallible, and he is at liberty to exercise it, different opinions will be formed. As long as the connection subsists between his reason and his self-love, his opinions and his passions will have a reciprocal influence on each other; and the former will be objects to which the latter will attach themselves. The diversity in the faculties of men, from which the rights of property originate, is not less an insuperable obstacle to a uniformity of interests. The protection of these faculties is the first object of Government. From the protection of different and unequal faculties of acquiring property, the possession of different degrees and kinds of property immediately results; and from the influence of these on the sentiments and views of the respective proprietors, ensues a division of the society into different interests and parties.

The latent causes of faction are thus sown in the nature of man; and we see them everywhere brought into different degrees of activity, according to the different circumstances of civil society. A zeal for different opinions concerning religion, concerning Government, and many other points, as well of speculation as of practice; an attachment to different leaders ambitiously contending for pre-eminence and power; or to persons of other descriptions whose fortunes have been interesting to the human passions, have in turn divided mankind into parties, inflamed them with mutual animosity, and rendered them much more disposed to vex and oppress each other, than to co-operate for their common good. So strong is this propensity of mankind to fall into mutual animosities, that where no substantial occasion presents itself, the most frivolous and fanciful distinctions have been sufficient to kindle their unfriendly passions, and excite their most violent conflicts. But the most common and durable source of factions has been the various and unequal distribution of property. Those who hold and those who are without property have ever formed distinct interests in society. Those who are creditors, and those who are debtors, fall under a like discrimination. A landed interest, a manufacturing interest, a mercantile interest, a moneyed interest, with many lesser interests, grow up of necessity in civilized nations, and divide them into different classes, actuated by different sentiments and views. The regulation of these various and interfering interests forms the principal task of modern Legislation, and involves the spirit of party and faction in the necessary and ordinary operations of Government.

No man is allowed to be judge in his own cause, because his interest would certainly bias his judgment and, not improbably, corrupt his integrity. With equal, nay with greater reason, a body of men are unfit to be both judges and parties at the same time; yet what are many of the most important acts of legislation but so many judicial determinations, not indeed concerning the rights of single persons, but concerning the rights of large bodies of citizens; and what are the different classes of legislators but advocates and parties to the causes which they determine? Is a law proposed concerning private debts? It is a question to which the creditors are parties on one side and the debtors on the other. Justice ought to hold the balance between them. Yet the parties are, and must be, themselves the judges; and the most numerous party, or in other words, the most powerful faction must be expected to prevail. Shall domestic manufacturers be encouraged, and in what degree, by restrictions on foreign manufacturers? are questions which would be differently decided by the landed and the manufacturing classes, and probably by neither with a sole regard to justice and the public good. The apportionment of taxes on the various descriptions of property is an act which seems to require the most exact impartiality; yet there is, perhaps, no legislative act in which greater opportunity and temptation are given to a predominant party to trample on the rules of justice. Every shilling with which they overburden the inferior number is a shilling saved to their own pockets.

It is in vain to say that enlightened statesmen will be able to adjust these clashing interests and render them all subservient to the public good. Enlightened statesmen will not always be at the helm. Nor, in many cases, can such an adjustment be made at all without taking into view indirect and remote considerations, which will rarely prevail over the immediate interest which one party may find in disregarding the rights of another or the good of the whole.

The inference to which we are brought is that the *causes* of faction cannot be removed and that relief is only to be sought in the means of controlling its *effects*.

If a faction consists of less than a majority, relief is supplied by the republican principle, which enables the majority to defeat its sinister views by regular vote. It may clog the administration, it may convulse the society; but it will be unable to execute and mask its violence under the forms of the Constitution. When a majority is included in a faction, the form of popular government, on the other hand, enables it to sacrifice to its ruling passion or interest both the public good and the rights of other citizens. To secure the public good and private rights against the danger of such a faction, and at the same time to preserve the spirit and the form of popular government, is then the great object to which our enquiries are directed. Let me add that it is the great desideratum by which alone this form of government can be rescued from the opprobrium under which it has so long labored and be recommended to the esteem and adoption of mankind.

By what means is this object attainable? Evidently by one of two only. Either the existence of the same passion or interest in a majority at the same time must be prevented, or the majority, having such co-existent passion or interest, must be rendered, by their number and local situation, unable to concert and carry into effect schemes of oppression. If the impulse and the opportunity be suffered to coincide, we well know that neither moral nor religious motives can be relied on as an adequate control. They are not found to be such on the injustice and violence of individuals, and lose their efficacy in proportion to the number combined together, that is, in proportion as their efficacy becomes needful.

From this view of the subject it may be concluded that a pure Democracy, by which I mean a Society consisting of a small number of citizens, who assemble and administer the Government in person, can admit of no cure for the mischiefs of faction. A common passion or interest will, in almost every case, be felt by a majority of the whole; a communication and concert results from the form of Government itself; and there is nothing to check the inducements to sacrifice the weaker party or an obnoxious individual. Hence it is that such Democracies have ever been spectacles of turbulence and contention; have ever been found incompatible with personal security or the rights of property; and have in general been as short in their lives as they have been violent in their deaths. Theoretic politicians, who have patronized this species of Government, have erroneously supposed that by reducing mankind to a perfect equality in their political rights, they would at the same time be perfectly equalized and assimilated in their possessions, their opinions, and their passions.

A Republic, by which I mean a Government in which the scheme of representation takes place, opens a different prospect and promises the cure for which we are seeking. Let us examine the points in which it varies from pure Democracy, and we shall comprehend both the nature of the cure and the efficacy which it must derive from the Union.

The two great points of difference between a Democracy and a Republic are: first, the delegation of the Government, in the latter, to a small number of citizens elected by the rest; secondly, the greater number of citizens and greater sphere of country over which the latter may be extended.

The effect of the first difference is, on the one hand, to refine and enlarge the public views by passing them through the medium of a chosen body of citizens, whose wisdom may best discern the true interest of their country and whose patriotism and love of justice will be least likely to sacrifice it to temporary or partial considerations. Under such a regulation it may well happen that the public voice, pronounced by the representatives of the people, will be more consonant to the public good than if pronounced by the people themselves, convened for the purpose. On the other hand, the effect may be inverted. Men of factious tempers, of local prejudices, or of sinister designs, may, by intrigue, by corruption, or by other means, first obtain the suffrages, and then betray the interests of the people. The question resulting is, whether small or extensive Republics are most favorable to the election of proper guardians of the public weal; and it is clearly decided in favor of the latter by two obvious considerations.

In the first place it is to be remarked that however small the Republic may be, the Representatives must be raised to a certain number in order to guard against the cabals of a few; and that however large it may be they must be limited to a certain number in order to guard against the confusion of a multitude. Hence, the number of Representatives in the two cases not being in proportion to that of the Constituents, and being proportionally greatest in the small Republic, it follows that if the proportion of fit characters be not less in the large than in the small Republic, the former will present a greater option, and consequently a greater probability of a fit choice.

In the next place, as each Representative will be chosen by a greater number of citizens in the large than in the small Republic, it will be more difficult for unworthy candidates to practise with success the vicious arts by which elections are too often carried; and the suffrages of the people being more free, will be more likely to centre on men who possess the most attractive merit and the most diffusive and established characters.

It must be confessed that in this, as in most other cases, there is a mean, on both sides of which inconveniencies will be found to lie. By enlarging too much the number of electors, you render the representative too little acquainted with all their local circumstances and lesser interests; as by reducing it too much, you render him unduly attached to these, and too little fit to comprehend and pursue great and national objects. The Federal Constitution forms a happy combination in this respect; the great and aggregate interests being referred to the national, the local and particular to the State legislatures.

The other point of difference is the greater number of citizens and extent of territory which may be brought within the compass of Republican than of Democratic Government; and it is this circumstance principally which renders factious combinations less to be dreaded in the former than in the latter. The smaller the society, the fewer probably will be the distinct parties and interests composing it; the fewer the distinct parties and interests, the more frequently will a majority be found of the same party; and the smaller the number of individuals composing a majority, and the smaller the compass within which they are placed, the more easily will they concert and execute their plans of oppression. Extend the sphere and you take in a greater variety of parties and interests; you make it less probable that a majority of the whole will have a common motive to invade the rights of other citizens; or if such a common motive exists, it will be more difficult for all who feel it to discover their own strength and to act in unison with each other. Besides other impediments, it may be remarked, that where there is a consciousness of unjust or dishonorable purposes, communication is always checked by distrust in proportion to the number whose concurrence is necessary.

Hence, it clearly appears that the same advantage which a Republic has over a Democracy in controlling the effects of faction is enjoyed by a large over a small republic—is enjoyed by the Union over the States composing it. Does this advantage consist in the substitution of representatives whose enlightened views and virtuous sentiments render them superior to local prejudices and to schemes of injustice? It will not be denied that the representation of the Union will be most likely to possess these requisite endowments. Does it consist in the greater security afforded by a greater variety of parties, against the event of any one party being able to outnumber and oppress the rest? In an equal degree does the increased variety of parties comprised within the Union increase this security? Does it, in fine, consist in the greater obstacles opposed to the concert and accomplishment of the secret wishes of an unjust and interested majority? Here again the extent of the Union gives it the most palpable advantage.

The influence of factious leaders may kindle a flame within their particular States but will be unable to spread a general conflagration through the other States: a religious sect may degenerate into a political faction in a part of the Confederacy; but the variety of sects dispersed over the entire face of it must secure the national Councils against any danger from that source: a rage for paper money, for an abolition of debts, for an equal division of property, or for any other improper or wicked project, will be less apt to pervade the whole body of the Union than a particular member of it; in the same proportion as such a malady is more likely to taint a particular county or district than an entire State.

In the extent and proper structure of the Union, therefore, we behold a republican remedy for the diseases most incident to Republican Government. And according to the degree of pleasure and pride we feel in being republicans ought to be our zeal in cherishing the spirit and supporting the character of federalist.

PUBLIUS

NO. 51: MADISON

To what expedient, then, shall we finally resort, for maintaining in practice the necessary partition of power among the several departments as laid down in the constitution? The only answer that can be given is that as all these exterior provisions are found to be inadequate the defect must be supplied, by so contriving the interior structure of the government as that its several constituent parts may, by their mutual relations, be the means of keeping each other in their proper places. Without presuming to undertake a full development of this important idea I will hazard a few general observations which may perhaps place it in a clearer light, and enable us to form a more correct judgment of the principles and structure of the government planned by the convention.

In order to lay a due foundation for that separate and distinct exercise of the different powers of government, which to a certain extent is admitted on all hands to be essential to the preservation of liberty, it is evident that each department should have a will of its own; and consequently should be so constituted that the members of each should have as little agency as possible in the appointment of the members of the others. Were this principle rigorously adhered to, it would require that all the appointments for the supreme executive, legislative, and judiciary magistracies should be drawn from the same fountain of authority, the people, through channels having no communication whatever with one another. Perhaps such a plan of constructing the several departments would be less difficult in practice than it may in contemplation appear. Some difficulties, however, and some additional expense would attend the execution of it. Some deviations, therefore, from the principle must be admitted. In the constitution of the judiciary department in particular, it might be inexpedient to insist rigorously on the principle: first, because peculiar qualifications being essential in the members, the primary consideration ought to be to select that mode of choice which best secures these qualifications; second, because the permanent tenure by which the appointments are held in that department must soon destroy all sense of dependence on the authority conferring them.

It is equally evident that the members of each department should be as little dependent as possible on those of the others for the emoluments annexed to their offices. Were the executive magistrate, or the judges, not independent of the legislature in this particular, their independence in every other would be merely nominal.

But the great security against a gradual concentration of the several powers in the same department consists in giving to those who administer each department the necessary constitutional means and personal motives to resist encroachments of the others. The provision for defence must in this, as in all other cases, be made commensurate to the danger of attack. Ambition must be made to counteract ambition. The interest of the man must be connected with the constitutional rights of the place. It may be a reflection on human nature that such devices should be necessary to control the abuses of government. But what is government itself but the greatest of all reflections on human nature? If men were angels, no government would be necessary. If angels were to govern men, neither external nor internal controls on government would be necessary. In framing a government which is to be administered by men over men, the great difficulty lies in this: You must first enable the government to control the governed; and in the next place oblige it to control itself. A dependence on the people is, no doubt, the primary control on the government; but experience has taught mankind the necessity of auxiliary precautions.

This policy of supplying, by opposite and rival interests, the defect of better motives, might be traced through the whole system of human affairs, private as well as public. We see it particularly displayed in all the subordinate distributions of power, where the constant aim is to divide and arrange the several offices in such a manner as that each may be a check on the other; that the private interest of every individual may be a sentinel over the public rights. These inventions of prudence cannot be less requisite in the distribution of the supreme powers of the State.

But it is not possible to give to each department an equal power of self-defense. In republican government, the legislative authority necessarily predominates. The remedy for this inconveniency is to divide the legislature into different branches; and to render them, by different modes of election and different principles of action, as little connected with each other as the nature of their common functions and their common dependence on the society will admit. It may even be necessary to guard against dangerous encroachments by still further precautions. As the weight of the legislative authority requires that it should be thus divided, the weakness of the executive may require, on the other hand, that it should be fortified. An absolute negative on the legislature appears, at first view, to be the natural defense with which the executive magistrate should be armed. But perhaps it would be neither altogether safe nor alone sufficient. On ordinary occasions it might not be exerted with the requisite firmness, and on extraordinary occasions it might be perfidiously abused. May not this defect of an absolute negative be supplied by some qualified connection between this weaker branch of the stronger department, by which the latter may be led to support the constitutional rights of the former, without being too much detached from the rights of its own department?

If the principles on which these observations are founded be just, as I persuade myself they are, and they be applied as a criterion to the several State constitutions, and to the federal Constitution, it will be found that if the latter does not perfectly correspond with them, the former are infinitely less able to bear such a test.

There are, moreover, two considerations particularly applicable to the federal system of America, which place that system in a very interesting point of view.

First. In a single republic, all the power surrendered by the people is submitted to the administration of a single government; and usurpations are guarded against by a division of the government into distinct and separate departments. In the compound republic of America, the power surrendered by the people is first divided between two distinct governments, and then the portion allotted to each subdivided among distinct and separate departments. Hence a double security arises to the rights of the people. The different governments will control each other, at the same time that each will be controlled by itself.

Second. It is of great importance in a republic not only to guard the society against the oppression of its rulers, but to guard one part of the society against the injustice of the other part. Different interests necessarily exist in different classes of citizens. If a majority be united by a common interest, the rights of the minority will be insecure. There are but two methods of providing against this evil: The one by creating a will in the community independent of the majority—that is, of the society itself; the other, by comprehending in the society so many separate descriptions of citizens as will render an unjust combination of a majority of the whole very improbable, if not impracticable. The first method prevails in all governments possessing an hereditary or self-appointed authority. This, at best, is but a precarious security; because a power independent of the society may as well espouse the unjust views of the major as the rightful interests of the minor party, and may possibly be turned against both parties. The second method will be exemplified in the federal republic of the United States. Whilst all authority in it will be derived from and dependent on the society, the society itself will be broken into so many parts, interests and classes of citizens, that the rights of individuals, or of the minority, will be in little danger from interested combinations of the majority. In a free government the security for civil rights must be the same as that for religious rights. It consists in the one case in the multiplicity of interests, and in the other in the multiplicity of sects. The degree of security in both cases will depend on the number of interests and sects; and this may be presumed to depend on the extent of country and number of people comprehended under the same government. This view of the subject must particularly recommend a proper federal system to all the sincere and considerate friends of republican government: Since it shows that in exact proportion as the territory of the Union may be formed into more circumscribed Confederacies, or States, oppressive combinations of a majority will be facilitated; the best security, under the republican form, for the rights of every class of citizens, will be diminished; and consequently the stability and independence of some member of the government, the only other security, must be proportionally increased. Justice is the end of government. It is the end of civil society. It ever has been and ever will be pursued until it be obtained, or until liberty be lost in the pursuit. In a society under the forms of which the stronger faction can readily unite and oppress the weaker, anarchy may as truly be said to reign as in a state of nature, where the weaker individual is not secured against the violence of the stronger: And as, in the latter state, even the stronger individuals are prompted, by the uncertainty of their condition, to submit to a government which may protect the weak as well as themselves: So, in the former state, will the more powerful factions or parties be gradually induced, by a like motive, to wish for a government which will protect all parties, the weaker as well as the more powerful. It can be little doubted that if the State of Rhode Island was separated from the Confederacy and left to itself, the insecurity of rights under the popular form of government within such narrow limits would be displayed by such reiterated oppressions of factious majorities that some power altogether independent of the people would soon be called for by the voice of the very factions whose misrule had proved the necessity of it. In the extended republic of the United States, and among the great variety of interests, parties, and sects which it embraces, a coalition of a majority of the whole society could seldom take place on any other principles than those of justice and the general good; and there being thus less danger to a minor from the will of the major party, there must be less pretext, also, to provide for the security of the former, by introducing into the government a will not dependent on the latter, or, in other words, a will independent of the society itself. It is no less certain than it is important, notwithstanding the contrary opinions which have been entertained, that the larger the society, provided it lie within a practicable sphere, the more duly capable it will be of self-government. And happily for the *republican cause*, practicable sphere may be carried to a very great extent by a judicious modification and mixture of the *federal principle*.

PUBLIUS

FURTHER READING

Ackerman, Bruce. *We the People: Foundations.* Harvard University Press, 1993.

Amar, Akhil Reed. *America's Constitution: A Biography.* Random House, 2006.

Baer, Judith A. *Our Lives Before the Law: Constructing a Feminist Jurisprudence.* Princeton University Press, 1999.

Balkin, Jack M. *What* Brown v. Board of Education *Should Have Said: America's Top Legal Experts Rewrite America's Landmark Civil Rights Decision.* New York University Press, 2001.

Balkin, Jack M. *What* Roe v. Wade *Should Have Said: America's Top Legal Experts Rewrite America's Most Controversial Decision.* New York University Press, 2005.

Breyer, Stephen. *Active Liberty: Interpreting Our Democratic Constitution.* Vintage Books, 2006.

Breyer, Stephen. *Making Our Democracy Work: A Judge's View.* Knopf, 2010.

Dahl, Robert A. *How Democratic Is the American Constitution?* 2nd ed. Yale University Press, 2002.

Gillman, Howard. *The Constitution Besieged: The Rise and Demise of Lochner Era Police Powers Jurisprudence.* Duke University Press, 1993.

Gillman, Howard. *The Votes That Counted: How the Court Decided the 2000 Presidential Election.* University of Chicago Press, 2001.

Graber, Mark. *Dred Scott and the Problem of Constitutional Evil.* Cambridge University Press, 2006.

Hall, Kermit. *The Oxford Companion to American Law.* Oxford University Press, 2003.

Hall, Kermit. *The Oxford Companion to the Supreme Court of the United States.* 2nd ed., rev. Oxford University Press, 2005.

Ivers, Gregg, and Kevin T. McGuire. *Creating Constitutional Change: Clashes over Power and Liberty in the Supreme Court.* University of Virginia Press, 2004.

Levinson, Sanford. *Our Undemocratic Constitution: Where the Constitution Goes Wrong (and How We the People Can Begin Correcting It).* Oxford University Press, 2006.

Lewis, Anthony. *Freedom for the Thought That We Hate: A Biography of the First Amendment.* Basic Books, 2008.

Lewis, Anthony. *Gideon's Trumpet.* Random House, 1964.

McCloskey, Robert G., and Sanford Levinson. *The American Supreme Court.* University of Chicago Press, 2005.

Rehnquist, William H. *All the Laws But One: Civil Liberties in Wartime.* Knopf, 1998.

Ritter, Gretchen. *The Constitution as Social Design: Gender and Civic Membership in the American Constitutional Order.* Stanford University Press, 2006.

Scalia, Antonin. *A Matter of Interpretation: Federal Courts and the Law.* Princeton University Press, 1998.

Simon, James F. *What Kind of Nation: Thomas Jefferson, John Marshall, and the Epic Struggle to Create a United States.* Simon & Schuster, 2003.

Wood, Gordon S. *The Creation of the American Republic, 1776–1787.* University of North Carolina Press, 1982.

RECOMMENDED WEBSITES

The American Civil Liberties Union   www.aclu.org
The ACLU is committed to protecting the freedoms found in the Bill of Rights for all individuals. This sometimes controversial organization continuously monitors the government for violations of liberty and encourages its members to take political action.

Archiving Early America   www.earlyamerica.com
Americans during the Revolutionary War possessed a variety of competing ideals, principles, and interests. Visit this website to learn more about the early colonists and the founding of our government.

Concourts   www.concourts.net
The U.S. Supreme Court has the responsibility to examine and interpret the Constitution. The Concourts website assumes a comparative perspective and looks at the system of constitutional review in over 150 different countries.

Constitution Finder   http://confinder.richmond.edu/
Is the American Constitution a model for the world? Explore the constitutions of many different nations and see what elements of the U.S. Constitution can be found in the governing documents of other countries.

Electronic Privacy Information Center   http://epic.org/privacy
For an extensive list of privacy issues, go to the web page for the Electronic Privacy Information Center. Here you will find civil liberties concerns as they relate to all forms of information technology, including the Internet.

FindLaw   http://findlaw.com/casecode/state.html
The FindLaw website provides a list of all fifty state constitutions. Click on your state and try to identify such constitutional principles as bicameralism, staggered terms of office, checks and balances, or separation of powers.

Freedom Forum   www.freedomforum.org
Freedom of speech and freedom of the press are considered critical in any democracy; however, only some kinds of speech are fully protected against restrictions. Freedom Forum is a nonpartisan agency that investigates and analyzes such First Amendment restrictions.

The Free Expression Network   www.FREEExpression.org
The First Amendment is the bedrock of freedom in the United States. The Free Expression Network is an organization "dedicated to preserving the right to free expression," and on their website you can find links to important First Amendment issues and organizations.

The National Archives   www.archives.gov/
This government site provides information about and actual digital images of such founding documents as the Declaration of Independence, the U.S. Constitution, and the Bill of Rights.

The National Constitution Center   www.constitutioncenter.org
The National Constitution Center in Philadelphia maintains a website that provides in-depth instructional analysis of the U.S. Constitution. Check out the Interactive Constitution function and follow the document from its Preamble through the Twenty-Seventh Amendment.

Oyez   www.oyez.com
This website for U.S. Supreme Court media has a great search engine to find information on cases affecting civil liberties like *Lemon v. Kurtzman, Miranda v. Arizona, Mapp v. Ohio*, and *New York Times Co. v. Sullivan*, to name a few.

The PBS *Liberty!* Series   www.pbs.org/ktca/liberty
The PBS *Liberty!* series on the American Revolution offers an in-depth look at the Revolutionary War and includes information on historical events including the Constitutional Convention.

The Religious Freedom Page   http://religiousfreedom.lib.virginia.edu/
The establishment clause of the U.S. Constitution has been interpreted to mean a "wall of separation" between government and religion. On the Religious Freedom page you can find information on a variety of issues pertaining to religious freedom in the United States and around the world.

The Supreme Court of the United States   www.supremecourtus.gov
The website for the U.S. Supreme Court provides information on recent decisions. Take a moment to read some oral arguments, briefs, or court opinions.

INDEX

homosexuality, 25–26, 43
House of Representatives. *See also* Congress
 constitution and powers of, 7–9
 differences between Senate and, 8
 elections to, 10
 powers and terms of, 6

impeachment, 7, 9, 20, 22, 23
income taxes, 51–52
industrialization, 15
interstate commerce, 14–15

Jackson, Andrew, 15, 29
Jay, John, 75
J.E.B. v. Alabama ex rel. T. B. (1994), 62
Jefferson, Thomas, 21, 32, 46, 62, 63
Johnson, Andrew, 9, 22
Johnson, William Samuel, 4
journals, 10–11
judicial branch
 checks and balances and, 5
 jurisdiction of, 23–24
 power and tenure of office in, 6, 22–23
 restrictions of powers in, 33, 45
judicial review, 1, 22, 61
juries
 in civil cases, 41–42
 as Constitutional provision, 61–62
 in criminal cases, 39

Kelo v. City of New London (2005), 40–41
Kent v. Dulles (1958), 62
Kimel v. Florida Board of Regents (2000), 45
King, Martin Luther, Jr., 63
King, Rufus, 4
Kyollo v. United States (2001), 38

Lawrence v. Texas (2003), 43
laws
 approval and signatures for, 5
 equal protection of, 47–49
 ex post facto laws, 17, 32
 passing, 12–13
legislative branch. *See also* Congress
 checks and balances and, 5
 powers and terms of, 6
 powers of, 4–5, 23

Lewis, John, 2
libel, 36–37
liberty, loss of, 16–17
Lincoln, Abraham, 16
liquor, prohibition of, 52–53, 55–56
Luther v. Borden (1849), 27

Madison, James, 4, 5, 30, 33, 75–84
Mapp v. Ohio (1961), 38
Marbury v. Madison (1803), 22
marriage, 25–26
Marshall, John, 14
Martin v. Hunter's Lessee (1816), 22
Mason, George, 30
McCain-Feingold Act (2002), 36
McDonald v. Chicago (2010), 37
Melendez-Diaz v. Massachusetts (2009), 41
Military Commissions Act (2006), 16
military resources, 37
militias, 37
Minor v. Happersett (1875), 53
Miranda v. Arizona (1966), 39
Moose Lodge v. Irvis (1972), 48
Morris, Gouverneur, 4

national government
 limits on, 33
 powers of, 6, 13–17
National Prohibition Cases (1920), 53
national supremacy, 6
national unity and power, 6
"New Deal Consensus," 15
New Deal programs, 15, 23
"New Jersey Plan," 7
New York Times Co. v. Sullivan (1964), 36–37
New York v. United States (1992), 44
Nineteenth Amendment, 53
Ninth Amendment, 43
Nixon, Richard, 22
nobility, titles of, 16, 17, 32
nullification, 29

Oath of Office, 19
oaths, for political officials, 29
Obama, Barack, 15, 19, 36, 60
obscene speech, 36
oversight, 18